Floral Patterns

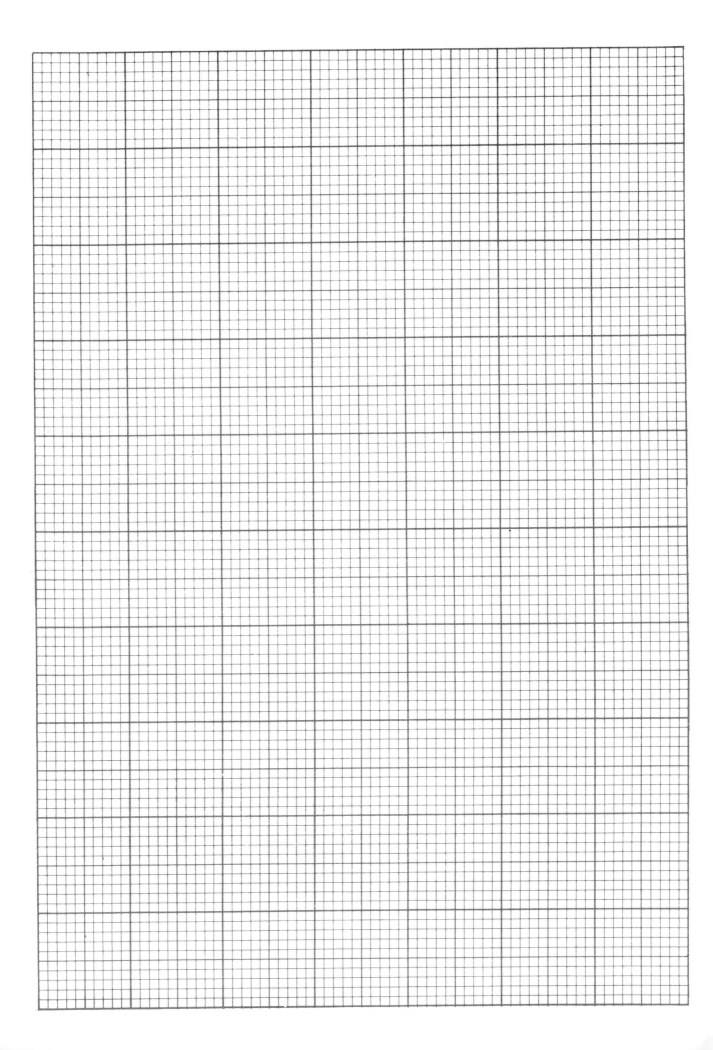

Floral Patterns

for Needlecraft and the Decorative Arts

Karen E. Oleson

VNR VAN NOSTRAND REINHOLD COMPANY
New York Cincinnati Toronto London Melbourne

Copyright © 1978 by Litton Educational Publishing, Inc.
Library of Congress Catalog Card Number 77-19324
ISBN 0-442-26282-5

Printed in the United States of America.
Designed by Loudan Enterprise

Published in 1978 by Van Nostrand Reinhold Company
A division of Litton Educational Publishing, Inc.
135 West 50th Street, New York, N.Y. 10020, U.S.A.

Van Nostrand Reinhold Limited
1410 Birchmount Road
Scarborough, Ontario M1P 2E7, Canada

Van Nostrand Reinhold Australia Pty. Ltd.
17 Queen Street
Mitcham, Victoria 3132, Australia

Van Nostrand Reinhold Company Limited
Molly Millars Lane
Wokingham, Berkshire, England

16 15 14 13 12 11 10 9 8 7 6 5 4 3 2 1

Library of Congress Cataloging in Publication Data
Oleson, Karen E.
    Floral patterns for needlecraft and the decora-
tive arts.

    Bibliography: p.
    Includes index.
1. Needlework—Patterns.   2. Design, Decorative—Plant forms.   I. Title.
TT753.042   746.4'4   77-19324
ISBN 0-442-26282-5 pbk.

Contents

Acknowledgments

Whenever you work on a project of this size, there are usually so many people who have influenced and guided you that to recognize each one individually is very difficult. However, there are always several people who are particularly influential.

First, I thank Alan Deighton, a very special friend, his wife, and his son Simon, who, over the past ten years, have all expressed warm encouragement and assistance in both my business and personal life. They have all shown me hospitality, produced the finest of art transfers, and exhibited that special relationship between craftsmen which shows no national boundaries. Alan Deighton and his family live in the North Devon countryside of England. Simon Deighton is listed under Suppliers.

Finally, I thank Mildred Davis, who resides in Chestnut Hill, Massachusetts. Over the years, she has been the warmest friend and has most influenced my own style and development. If it had not been for this very special person, I know that the others would not have succeeded in convincing me to do this book. This year Mildred has started a new Textile Institute in connection with Pine Manor College in Chestnut Hill, Massachusetts, which will, without question, bring her special talents to more budding needlework and textile artisans than ever before. How lucky I feel to have known her.

The drawings within this book have been researched and adapted from a wide variety of resources including seed catalogs, life studies in the countryside of New Hampshire, my drawings from the past twenty years of classes and notebooks, and from the following publications which are represented in separate sections:

Mountain Flowers in Color by Anthony Huxley. Illustrations by Daphne Barry and Mary Grierson. Copyright © 1967 Blandford Press Ltd., England. Adaptations with permission of Macmillan Publishing Co., Inc. and Blandford Press Ltd., England.

Adaptations of Mary Vaux Walcott watercolors by permission from the National Collection of Fine Arts, Smithsonian Institution, Washington, D.C. Reproductions of the watercolors used within this book may be found in Walcott's *North American Wildflowers*, published by the Smithsonian Institution.

The section on the Millefleur tapestries includes a number of background flowers which can be seen in The Unicorn Tapestries. The best publication for color on these is *The Unicorn Tapestries* by Margaret B. Freeman published in 1976 by the Metropolitan Museum of Art, New York.

Some of the resource books used to verify the correct botanical shapes and sizes of the florals used are listed in the Bibliography. You will find them also useful for color selection.

To all other people who have had to put up with my "creative" streaks this past year, my thanks and appreciation for your understanding.

Introduction

Floral patterns are perhaps the single most popular and timeless theme used in the decorative arts. As far back as first recorded history, floral subjects—whether they be abstracted illustrations for the pure love of the plant or for symbolic reasons—have had special meaning to mankind. Realistic drawing of plants and flowers has developed into a fine art in the textile and art fields. In ceramics work, the development of floral motifs has come primarily through fine china painters in both the Orient and Europe. Is there any decorative art form which does not use florals as a central theme?

The purpose of this coloring and pattern book is to give you a vast resource of flower drawings. It provides guidelines for expanding your skills and creativity in the use of these illustration for needlework and, to a lesser degree, for other decorative crafts such as tole painting, ceramics, liquid embroidery, stenciling, etc.

The large illustrations are superimposed on a graph (ten squares to the inch) so that you can enlarge or reduce easily for specific projects. Instruction on how to do this simply is given in Chapter 2. In addition, the graph makes it easy to abstract the pattern further for counted-thread work such as canvas work, cross-stitch, and needlepoint. Instruction on how to do this is given in Chapter 3.

Most importantly, this book is intended to help you build confidence in developing your own individual projects. By using colored pencils, crayons, watercolors, pastels, or inks to color in the line drawings, you will develop your own sense of color. You can then take your completed, colored drawings to the store and pick out your supplies by matching the colors exactly.

How do you develop your own sense of color? I have been asked that so many times that I have lost count. Let me ask you a question in return. How did you pick out that favorite piece of clothing, drapery material, living-room picture, bed linen . . . ? Wasn't the color combination a very important part of its appeal to you? Go get it now and

look at the colors. What's wrong with using the same colors in your next project? Who said that a rose must be yellow, pink, red, or white? If you look at wallpaper samples, you will find that roses are often blue, lavender, green, brown, and even gray. It's the colors you put together in the same piece that makes it work or not work. You can tell immediately whether your color choice is successful if you use this book as a workbook. If you are going to be unhappy with your color selection, how much better that you say "yuck" while it is still in the coloring book than after it is on your new vase or wall hanging. After starting a project, you have no way of changing your mind about the coloring without a major job of undoing what has already been worked. That in itself is a punishing experience. So, let your youthful coloring-book fantasies take off with this book and develop projects from your own exploration of color.

In Chapter 10 there are suggestions on how and where to use the illustrations. This is only the tip of the iceberg. By taking bits and pieces of the patterns and repositioning them in your own project, the possibilities are limitless. You can use these patterns literally for anything, from a tiny leaf and bud twined around the collar of a blouse to a mass of florals and vines on a double- or queen-sized bedspread.

For those of you who are not quite ready to dive in, the next chapters present specific instructions for basic steps from coloring the pattern through transferring it to an object or fabric. Stitches for needlework are provided in the Glossary of Stitches.

The following patterns represent a wide variety of plants and flowers; however, if I have left out your favorites, please let me know so that they can be included in future pattern books. I'd also be interested to know how you used these patterns and if there are other subjects for which you wish you had patterns, so feel free to write me c/o the publisher, Van Nostrand Reinhold Company.

CHAPTER 1:

Color

Before you begin work on your project, you must decide what colors to use and where to use them. By coloring the patterns in this book with crayons, pencils, or paints, you can experiment with different color combinations and develop your sense of taste. First, lightly color in all areas of the pattern. Then darken those areas you wish to shade and add contrasting colors where desired. Next to the colored pattern, color a sample box for each color and value you decide to use in the finished piece. This will give you a complete "key" for your pattern. When you go to the store, you can label each box with the manufacturer's number of the actual thread or paint you select. Then you will have a complete and permanent record of your project so that you can produce a second copy—even years later.

If you have developed a good sense of color and wish to jump ahead, turn to Fig. 3 at the end of this chapter. It will help you key the colors of your pencils used in this book with the manufacturer's color numbers for the supplies you intend to use. Color in Fig. 3 as indicated at the end of this chapter and have a permanent tool for supplies.

However, if you have no confidence in your ability to choose colors that work well together, a good way to begin is by finding a piece of fabric or wallpaper that you particularly like. On Fig. 1 color in all the different colors you find in your sample with the comparable color in your pencils or crayons. Keep the colors within the areas indicated. You now have a color scheme or palette of

colors that you can use in your first project.

Any combination of colors that you find pleasing can be a color palette and used in your work. The most basic palette consists of only one color which is called "monochrome." You can add interest to your piece by adding values (lighter and darker shades of the same color) and by adding texture

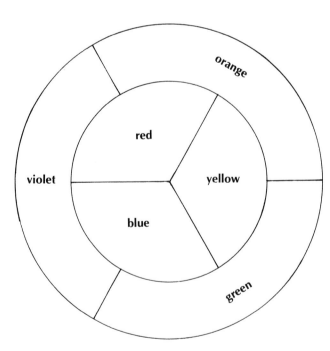

1. Basic color wheel. Color the primary colors (red, yellow, blue) and the secondary colors (violet, orange, green) with whatever you will be using in this book—colored pencils, ink, crayons, pastels, or paints.

through stitch selection or special brush techniques. If you choose to use the values in shaded techniques, the end effect is like a painting. If you contrast the values without regard to the picture, you have a stylized and designed effect. Texture can add a realistic or playful quality to the overall work. Much antique needlework and ceramics used monochrome techniques.

The other basic category is called "polychrome" which simply means many colors. This is where many of us lose confidence in our sense of taste. If you have colored in Fig. 1 as indicated earlier, it is now time to decide which type of color scheme (palette) you have selected so that you can duplicate the overall effect with other color combinations later.

Notice on Fig. 1 how the colors are laid out in two circles with each color either touching another or opposite to another color. In Fig. 2, use the same colors from Fig. 1 and color them in again. Now you have the colors adjacent to their nearest "relative" in the color wheel. The subject of color is huge and if you get intrigued, see the Bibliography for books that discuss this subject in depth.

Polychrome palettes break into several categories. The first is the analogous (or complementary) color scheme which is based on the principle that closely related colors harmonize. Any two colors adjacent to each other on the continuous color wheel in Fig. 2 will work well together. Again, you can add interest to your work by using different values of the two colors and by adding texture. See if your chosen color scheme is in this category.

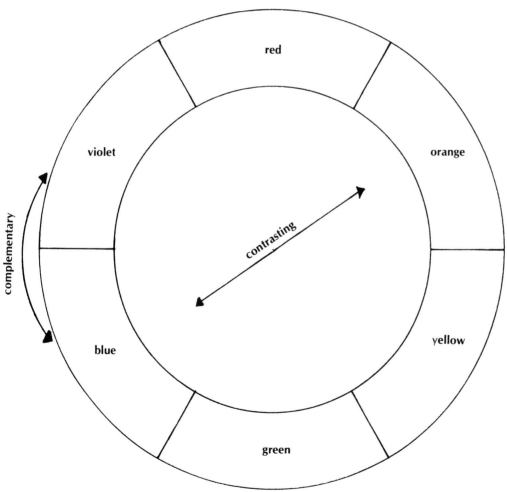

2. Continuous color wheel. Color this wheel with the same colors and materials chosen for the basic color wheel. Notice the progression from one color to the next: primary, secondary, primary, secondary, etc. Adjacent colors are called complementary; any two colors directly opposite each other are called contrasting.

The second basic color palette is based on the principle that contrasting colors also work well together. Any two colors that are opposite each other on the continuous color wheel in Fig. 2, therefore, can be used. Is your chosen color scheme filled with contrasting colors? Or have you found that most of your contrasting colors are only used for accent on an analogous color scheme?

Do you know more about what you like now? As you experiment, you will find many more combinations or palettes of color; the possibilities are limitless. The end result of your discoveries is called "your sense of taste." It is that simple. Each of us is different so no two of you will ever develop exactly the same taste in color and each piece you work will be distinctly different from anyone else in the world.

For those who are working in needlework, I have grouped different manufacturers' threads together into three basic palettes to help you get off the ground in the early stages of developing your own color sense. All the colors within one palette will blend well when used together whether you choose to use an analogous (or complementary) color scheme or a contrasting combination in your piece. How you balance these colors in one piece is where this coloring book will help develop your skills. Most of the colors given have five values which are listed from light to dark.

ANTIQUE PALETTE

This is a series of muted colors reminiscent of the early Colonial period when materials were colored with vegetable dyes. You may find this selection most appropriate for a truly naturalistic look. You can revise this listing to include or eliminate any of the choices and substitute anything that pleases your own sense of color.

Color Name	Paternayan Crewel or Tapestry Yarn	DMC 6-stranded Cotton (Mouline Special)
1. blue	747, 737, 727, 717, 707	775, 794, 793, 792, 791
2. chocolate	996, 986, 976, 966, 956	842, 841, 840, 839, 838
3. blue-green	945, 940, 938, 918, 908	504, 503, 502, 501, 500
4. sage green	943, 942, 923, 922, 912	n/a, n/a, 3053, 3054, 3051
5. old gold	941, 459, 449, 439, 429	3047, 834, 833, 832, 831
6. purple	634, 628, 624, 614, 608	453, 3042, 3041, 327, n/a
7. rose	835, 830, 825, 820, 815	948, 758, 356, 355, 902
8. gray	152, 146, 142, 122, 106	648, 647, 646, 645, 844

BASIC PALETTE

Those colors most commonly used in the American home and illustrated in our magazines are found within this color scheme. They are brighter and more intense than those in the antique palette but less so than the colors in the primary palette. Again, this selection is suitable for traditional florals and will give them the brightness of a spring or summer day.

Color Name	Paternayan Crewel or Tapestry Yarn	DMC 6-stranded Cotton (Mouline Special)
1. light blue	735, 730, 725, 720, 715	747, 519, 518, 517, n/a
2. golden brown	160, 150, 135, 130, 125	ecru, 612, 611, 610, 3031
3. tree brown	491, 481, 473, 471, 463	822, 644, 642, 640, (3031)
4. bright yellow-green	925, 920, 915, 910, 905	472, 471, 470, 469, 937
5. olive green	947, 933, 927, 917, n/a	(472), 581, 580, 936, n/a
6. carnation red	296, 276, 246, 226, 216, 206	963, 894, 893, 892, 891, 321
7. yellow	475, 470, 465, 460, 415	746, 3078, 727, 726, 725
8. plum	635, 630, 625, 605, n/a	554, 553, 552, 550
9. gray	152, 146, 142, 122, 106	648, 647, 646, 645, 844

PRIMARY PALETTE

This palette is comprised of primary and secondary colors with a few additions to round out the possibilities. These colors are used most often in the primitive work of children and in contemporary homes where ultra modern furnishings and strong angles cry out for brilliant color. The less traditional person who loves traditional floral patterns used in a highly unconventional way should try these color combinations.

Color Name	Paternayan Crewel or Tapestry Yarn	DMC 6-stranded Cotton (Mouline Special)
1. royal blue	353, 351, 343, 341, 333, 331	800, 809, 799, 798, 797, 820
2. tree brown	491, 481, 473, 471, 463	822, 644, 642, 640, 3031
3. apple green	944, 934, 924, 914, n/a	no comparable color
4. bright green	567, 557, 547, 517, n/a, n/a	704, 703, 702, 701, 700, 699
5. peacock green	548, 544, 538, 518, 514, n/a	955, 954, 913, 912, 911, 910, 909
6. buttercup	451, 431, 421, 417	945, 744, 743, 742
7. orange	(substitute for apple green)	741, 740
8. royal purple	657, 647, 637, 627, 617	211, 210, 209, 208, 327
9. red	292, 290, 268, 218, 208	957, 956, 321, 498, 815

DESIGNING YOUR OWN PALETTE

Fig. 3 is a complete color wheel with the inner circle for your pencil colors (lightest values to the center and darkest to the outside) with a matching box in the outermost circle to place your manufacturer's color number for the thread or paint you intend to use. Notice that within any of the color areas you have room for at least three different colors within that basic color range. The possibilities for your own palettes are limitless and up to you. Remember that contrasting colors work well as accents in analogous color schemes. If you are going to remember to pick up the right thread color, you will need to put in contrasting colors on your wheel even though you don't intend to use much of them in your finished piece. Place your browns and grays outside the color wheel and add the manufacturer's numbers under them or beside them as a separate project. It is the basic color wheel that will need your closest attention in color selection.

3. Color wheel worksheet. Color the inside five rings with the same materials used for Figs. 1 and 2. There are spaces for three different colors in each color family and five different values of each color. When you go to the store to purchase your supplies, note in the outside five rings the manufacturer's color number for the shade and value you are purchasing for the corresponding spaces in the inner ring. Then use this worksheet for determining what supplies to buy for each project. Place your browns and grays outside the color wheel and add the manufacturer's color numbers next to them.

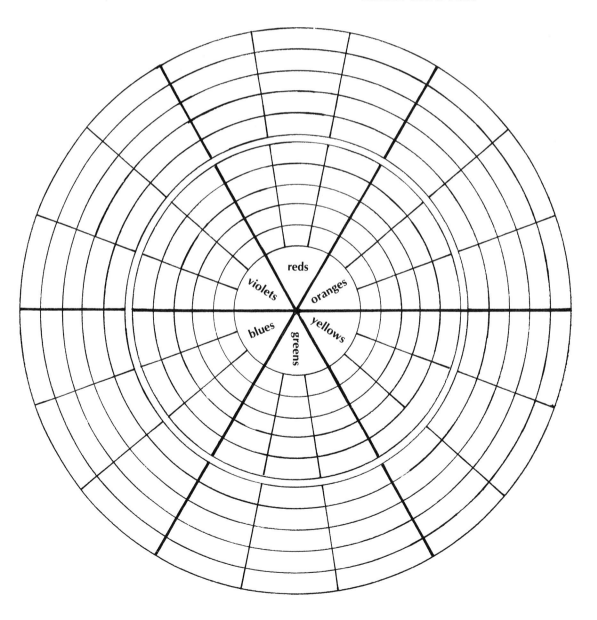

CHAPTER 2:

Enlarging and Reducing Patterns

There are a number of very simple techniques for enlarging and reducing patterns and designs. Your local printer undoubtedly has an enlarging camera and for a small fee can blow up or reduce the drawing to exactly the size you wish. In addition, there is a wonderful gadget available called a pantograph that attaches to your pencil and table. You set the arm for the degree of enlargement or reduction desired and as you trace the drawing, the pantograph retraces it on another piece of paper in the new size. This tool is available through local stationery and art supply stores.

All the patterns in this book are superimposed on a 10-squares-to-the-inch graph. You can enlarge or reduce an illustration by redrawing it square for square on a different sized graph. For example, if you use an 8-squares-to-the-inch or 4-squares-to-the-inch graph you will enlarge the pattern proportionately. To reduce a drawing, use a smaller grid, such as 12-squares-to-the-inch or 16-squares-to-the-inch.

If you are a canvas-work or counted-thread specialist, you can achieve the same result without redrawing the pattern. Just change the mesh of your fabric. Any mesh which is larger in threads per inch than the 10-squares-per-inch graph will reduce the patterns. Those who do cross-stitch should remember that it takes two threads for one stitch. Fabric with 20 threads per inch will give you the same size pattern as shown in this book. More threads per inch will reduce the pattern; fewer will enlarge the pattern.

There are many books available on how to enlarge and reduce patterns and you may find them useful if you are changing the size of many of the patterns.

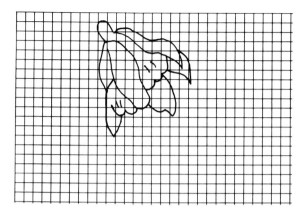

4. This drawing shows a segment of one pattern as it appears in this book on a 10-squares-to-the-inch graph.

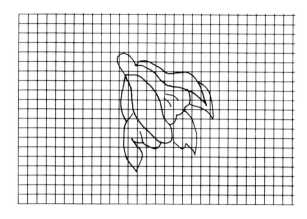

7. This is identical to Fig. 4

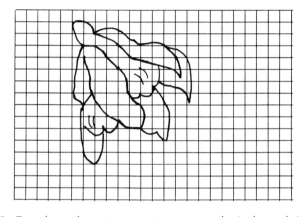

5. To enlarge the pattern, an 8-squares-to-the-inch graph is used and the design is redrawn by following the line from square to square in the top illustration.

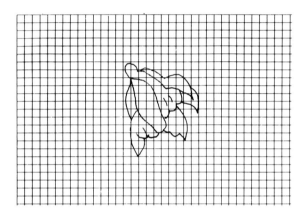

8. To reduce the pattern, redraw the line work on a smaller grid by following the lines square by square. This grid size is 12-squares-to-the-inch.

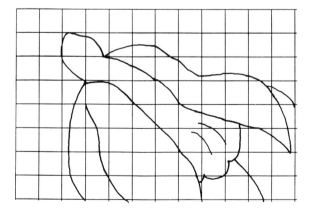

6. Further enlargement of the pattern is achieved here by using an even larger grid (4-squares-to-the-inch). You can accomplish the same results by having the line drawing enlarged commercially. When enlarged commercially, the lines of your drawing become coarser as they are enlarged further and further. If the lines become thick, you may find it helpful to redraw them with a pen.

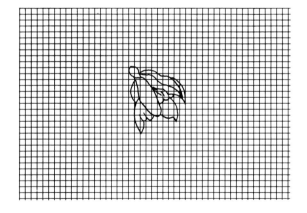

9. The graph here is 16-squares-to-the-inch. When reducing commercially, the lines of your drawing become finer as they are reduced further and further. If the lines become faint, you may want to darken them with a pen.

CHAPTER 3:

How to Transfer Patterns

No matter which medium you choose to use for the patterns in this book, you will need to redraw the pattern or trace it onto the object—fabric or clay for example—in order to proceed. Following are specific suggestions for crewel embroidery, canvas work and needlepoint, counted thread work, the painting arts, and the stencil arts.

However, one rule always prevails: the finest quality materials should be used. The finished piece will look better, be easier to work and will last indefinitely, and feel good to the touch. This is the "golden rule" of all artisans and craftsmen.

For the needle arts, the selection of fabric is dependent on the practical use for which the piece is intended. If, for example, you are going to use the finished piece for upholstery, then you will want a strong fabric that will last for many years. Your choice of threads would reflect the same need. If you intend to use the piece as a picture, then of course your selection can be less rigid.

CREWEL EMBROIDERY

The traditional fabrics for this wool-thread needlework are even-weave linen and linen twill. Flax, from which linen is made, is a tough vegetable fiber. Note that there are major differences between even-weave and counted-thread linen in the way the flax is twisted and in the way the fabric is woven. For crewel work, even-weave is desirable because your pattern can be transferred so that your fabric is squared off properly and your finished piece can be blocked well. Fabric that requires a high degree of expertise in the weaving will cost more. Thus, even-weave linen will be more expensive than the bumpy and irregular weave found in less carefully woven fabrics.

The reason for the traditional use of twill fabrics becomes obvious when you study the way the interwoven diagonal lines and fine threads of the fabric fold in around the needle and leave no hole in the fabric from either the needle or thread. In addition, the strength of the fabric has made it a favorite for upholstery, pillows, and screens. It will last through many generations in your family.

To transfer the patterns from this book onto your fabric, I suggest using dressmaker's carbon which is available in fabric stores. It protects your fabric and retains the line work. If your fabric is light in color, blue carbon will work nicely; if the color is very dark, such as is true of most denims, use the lightest color available—white if possible. Be sure your fabric is securely fastened on a hard surface so that it will not slip while you trace. You can cut out the page of this book or retrace it onto another sheet of paper. Use a sturdy paper such as vellum drawing or tracing paper.

With your fabric secured to a hard surface, place the drawing on the fabric in the exact place you wish it, and secure it with straight pins. Only now should you slip the dressmaker's carbon under the section you wish to trace first. Trace the drawing with a good ball-point pen or, if you are dexterous, use a tracing wheel. If you want to see how well the tracing is coming, just lift the carbon and peek, but be sure that you do not disturb the position of the pattern. When the tracing is complete, you can remove the pattern and dressmaker's carbon. You may want to go over the lines with a permanent line such as india ink provides. If the project is large and requires a lot of stitching, you may find this additional step helpful.

To retrace your pattern easily, use the new Mars

pen size 2 or 3. These are sold at local art supply stores. The line is fine enough to be covered by one very fine thread and will stay consistently wide in your redrawing. Do not use felt-tipped pens as they bleed into the fabric and their width is not easily controlled.

If you intend to use wool threads, which is the meaning of "crewel," use *only* permanent ink. You run a high risk with nonpermanent inks because they can stain your wools. If you are using cotton or linen threads, this requirement is not as crucial because they can be washed with detergents or sprayed with some of the new "wonder" chemicals to remove stains. Not all wools, however, will take this harsh treatment.

When you have (1) colored the pattern in the book, (2) selected the fabric you wish to use, (3) enlarged or reduced the pattern, and (4) traced the pattern onto the fabric and made the illustration permanent, you should consider stitch selection and texture. Chapter 4 shows the effect that different types of stitches have on the finished piece and illustrates both traditional interpretations of a design and the less conventional possibilities of stitch selection. All patterns can be done in quick-and-easy stitches or in highly complex and time-consuming possibilities. The choice is up to you. To help you expand your choices, the Glossary of Stitches gives a sampling of over eighty different stitches to consider.

At this point, you are ready to embroider your very own work of art. It is highly unlikely that anyone else will have a piece of needlework exactly like yours!

CANVAS WORK AND NEEDLEPOINT

There are two basic types of canvas and many sizes of mesh used for canvas work and needlepoint. Mono canvas has a single thread woven in both directions. The "hole for stitching" is placed equally in each direction on a given number of holes per inch—much like graph paper; these threads are called "mesh" instead of "grid." No. 10 mono canvas means there are ten threads per inch on the canvas.

The other basic type of canvas is penelope or double-mesh canvas in which there are two threads woven closely together between each stitching hole. In the traditional weave the horizontal threads are very close together and the vertical threads are slightly spread apart. This often causes a finished piece—particularly if it is circular in

nature—to look slightly askew, but proper blocking of the piece will align the threads into position.

The fibers used for canvas are numerous but the most common are cotton or linen. For those of you who do canvas work using many stitches besides the tent stitches, you will find an increasing flexibility in your stitching with No. 10 penelope canvas. By splitting the double threads as you work into 20 threads per inch, you can do petit point as well as vary your other stitches significantly in size and direction. Often penelope canvas is described as 10/20 penelope meaning that there are 10 stitches per inch unless the double threads are separated, in which case the number of stitches doubles.

There are three ways that the canvas worker can transfer a pattern to canvas: (1) by placing the design under the canvas and tracing the pattern, (2) by using the new transfer inks called Transpaints described below, and (3) by counting off the stitches from a graph. The last method is described fully under Counted Thread Work.

Tracing a pattern onto canvas can be fun and is very easy to do if you know a few "tricks." First trace the pattern onto tissue or tracing paper. Any paper that will allow light to pass through it from the back is suitable. You can use a bold marker or a heavy pencil for this. It is important that the line be dark and clear.

Now you must locate a substitute for a "light table." The best substitutes that I have found are a glass-topped table, which allows you to place a light on the floor beneath it, and a large glass window or door where daylight can be used as backlighting.

To transfer your design, you will also need the following materials: masking tape for anchoring your pattern and canvas, india ink and a very fine (000) sable brush or a Mars pen size 2 or 3 for outlining on the canvas, and either oil paints, which I prefer, or acrylics for coloring the outlined piece.

Secure the tissue tracing onto your glass surface. Be sure to tape down all four sides so that it won't shift just as you are transferring an intricate detail.

Next, take the piece of canvas, which should be at least four inches larger on each side than the pattern, and anchor it on top of the tracing with masking tape. Be sure that the squares of your canvas are horizontal and vertical to the pattern or you will be very frustrated when you stitch your design.

If you are using a glass-topped table, place a light

directly below the section you are tracing and proceed to draw on the canvas with india ink. Be sure your light source is directly under the section you are tracing. You will have to revise the pattern slightly as you trace so that it adjusts to the canvas mesh you have chosen. In canvas work you will always lose a percentage of the detail shown in the original design because of the geometric nature of this craft. The best results come from following the outlines of the large shapes first and then going back to add the details.

If you are using a glass window or door as a substitute for a light box, you will not be able to adjust your light source so try to work on a clear, bright day.

The traditional threads for canvas work and needlepoint are tapestry yarn and persian wool. The difference is quickly seen. Tapestry yarn looks quite similar to knitting yarn but is in fact a much stronger thread and the fiber specifications are quite different. Tapestry yarn can be used in rugs as well as needlepoint. Persian yarn is named after its origins in Persian carpets. It is made of three threads which are spun separately and then twisted together to give it bulk. In Oriental carpets the threads are then cut and the resulting pile is lush and full after the carpet has been stitched. The carpets are stitched with a series of knots (see turkey work in the Glossary of Stitches). Persian yarns can be used in canvas work as a single, double, or triple thread. This is by far the most versatile thread available for this artform. A single thread of persian wool is approximately the same weight as crewel yarn and can be substituted for crewel. Some manufacturers suggest that you split tapestry yarns to get a lighter weight thread for particular projects. Because this often weakens the thread, I do not suggest this approach. Tapestry yarns are lovely and most suitable for upholstery projects and rugs. If you need varying weights of thread for your project, use both tapestry yarn and persian wool. They will give entirely different effects to your work.

Silk, linen, and cotton threads are often used for highlighting and special effects in canvas work. If you are doing a delicate evening bag, you might consider stitching the entire piece in one of these threads as the overall effect is more delicate than with wools.

You may wish to explore the new Transpaint techniques and create your own transfer instead of tracing and hand painting directly on the canvas.

Transpaints are a new form of transfer ink available in twelve basic colors. They come with a formula book for color matching with Paternayan wools. By tracing the patterns in this book and then coloring them with these inks, you can iron the pattern directly onto your canvas. They are also helpful for counted thread work. (See Suppliers.) The following information is important to remember when using these textile transfer paints.

You should retrace the pattern onto a good bond or vellum paper. Follow the manufacturer's instructions on how to mix colors and match them to Paternayan wool colors. You can color the design by handpainting, airbrushing, or silk screening. Each of these techniques has advantages and disadvantages so read the manufacturer's information before deciding which to use. For most of us, handpainting is the answer.

It is most important that you use a very hard surface such as cardboard, masonite, or plywood under your canvas so that the pressure you apply (just the normal weight on your arm) to your iron is evenly distributed. You can use your household iron but it must be "bone dry." In addition, you should cover the painted transfer with aluminum foil so that the heat from your iron is spread evenly. Most steam irons have little holes on the bottom. Where there is a hole, there is a cold spot and the color will not transfer. The aluminum foil fills in these holes with heat.

A close relative to canvas work is counted thread embroidery which is distinguished by the careful charting of stitches. Instead of painting your pattern on the fabric to be stitched, a gridded graph is carefully counted out stitch by stitch and then the needlework is done directly on the unmarked fabric.

COUNTED THREAD WORK

No matter which type of counted thread work you choose—traditional cross-stitch or canvas work—the method of charting the colors and stitches is the same.

The illustrations in this book are superimposed on a gray, 10-squares-per-inch graph. You may choose to use the designs in this scale or to change the scale by redrawing the patterns onto a larger or smaller grid depending on whether you wish to further simplify the pattern or capture all the details of the original line work.

The selection of graph paper is one of the key choices to be made. If the pattern is detailed and you wish to capture all the detail possible, you may enlarge the pattern and then superimpose a 10-to-the-inch, or smaller, grid. The size of the end product will depend on the fabric mesh used.

If you wish to simplify and reduce the size of the pattern, superimpose a coarser grid such as 8-squares-to-the-inch and modify the line work as you retrace the design. You may find it easier to simply modify the patterns as you color them to make the line work follow the 10-to-the-inch grid behind each illustration.

The design in Fig. 10 has curved lines without regard to the grid behind it. In Fig. 11 the line work has been slightly adjusted to conform to the geometric nature of counted thread work. You can accomplish this redirection of line by using a colored pencil such as red and simply redrawing the line to suit the graph paper. If you are quick to read your graph paper, you can proceed directly to coloring the squares. Notice that the dotted lines which remain after the squares have been outlined represent the original lines of the drawing. Now that you have your bold outlines and details captured on the graph, begin to color the pattern.

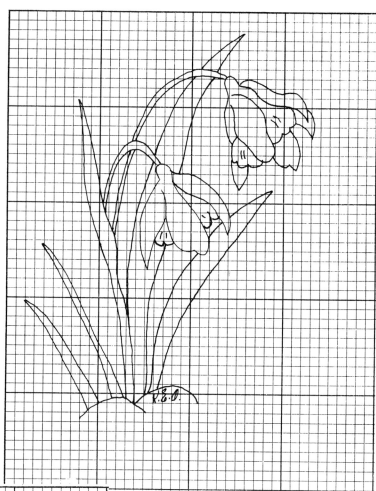

10. This pattern is reproduced here as it appears in this book except that the graph is more pronounced.

11. For counted thread work clarify the outlines of the appropriate squares by outlining the diameter of the boxes with a heavy marker or "squiggly" line.

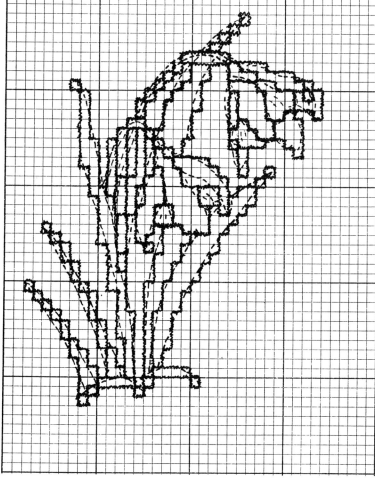

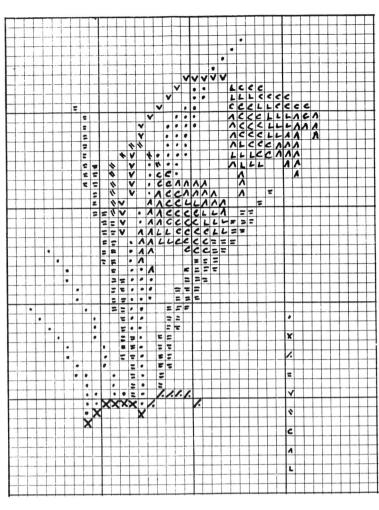

12. Fig. 10 is shown here as a chart of symbols. This is the traditional method used extensively in Europe. Each symbol represents a separate color. You would add the thread color numbers alongside the symbols to the right of the drawing for a permanent reference.

Fig. 12 shows the colors represented by symbols. This is the traditional method of graphing for counted thread work. At this point you should count carefully how many stitches wide and how many stitches deep your piece will be when finished. It is helpful to number the lines directly on the page so that you can note by a grid reference just where you leave off work. Note that every tenth horizontal and vertical line is heavier. Just mark every tenth line in one direction with a letter and with a number in the other direction—just like on a map.

Each square on the graph is one stitch on your fabric. In cross-stitch this means it represents a minimum of two threads in each direction. Linen fabric for counted-thread work is quoted as "threads per inch." If the count is 32 threads per inch, you will in cross-stitch have 16 stitches per inch by using two threads by two threads for each stitch. Should you choose to do Assisi embroidery, traditionally the cross-stitches are worked over three threads and your finished piece will be larger. You will then have approximately ten stitches per inch.

Suppose that you have 96 squares colored on your graph in one direction, and you have decided to do cross-stitches over two threads. On 32-threads-per-inch fabric you will have 16 stitches per inch. Your finished piece, therefore, will be six inches in width.

$$\frac{96 \text{ squares}}{16 \text{ stitches/inch}} = 6 \text{ inches}$$

You can see how the finished size of your piece is affected by your fabric count. The smaller the weave, the smaller your stitches must be and the smaller the finished piece will turn out.

The principle is exactly the same for canvas. However, if you are using the continental stitch or any of the tent stitches except the half-cross-stitch, you do not need to stitch over two or three threads;

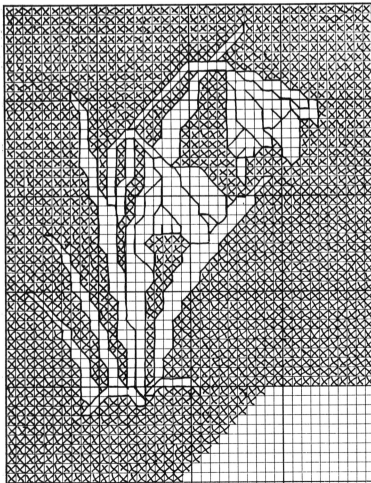

13. Assisi work is a counted thread technique in cross-stitch and back stitch or holbein stitch. Notice that with the use of back stitch, which is completed first, you can get softer angles and thinner lines than with traditional cross-stitch.

the mesh of the canvas will represent exactly the number of stitches per inch of the finished work. If you are working the half-cross-stitch, use penelope canvas. This fabric spells out the stitches per inch in the mesh count.

The traditional stitches used in counted thread work are the cross-stitch and the back stitch. Both are illustrated in the Glossary of Stitches. If you want the special effects obtainable from Assisi work, then redraw the pattern so that it is outlined and the background is filled in with cross-stitches.

Blackwork, whitework, and other counted thread techniques are also possible from the same techniques used for Assisi work. Instead of cross-stitches, however, you can choose many other stitches to both fill the design and the background.

PAINTING ARTS

The painting arts and crafts that are most suitable for pattern work include watercolor, ceramics, tole painting, and liquid embroidery. Each of these have different brush and pen techniques which are best explored in special books on each subject. Following are the techniques for transferring the design to the object you wish to decorate.

For watercolor the most useful method of transferring is to trace the pattern onto tracing paper. Make a self-carbon by applying graphite from your pencil to the backside of the drawing. Then place your tracing, graphite side down, onto watercolor paper and retrace the pattern. The graph is useful for drawing the pattern freehand.

The ceramics field is growing quickly and techniques for transferring are developing rapidly. I trace the patterns in pencil, graphite the backside of the traced drawing, and then retrace it with a ball point pen (accountant's very fine point) onto the ceramic ware. When working on greenware, this will leave an indentation which can easily be seen if the graphite is brushed off. On bisque, I find that retracing the graphite line with india ink and a fine Mars pen (size 0) helps retain the fine lines through the painting process. For china painting, refer to the publications of Bill Thompson and Doris Taylor and Anne Hart listed in the Bibliography. You can enlarge and reduce the patterns by the same methods used for needlework.

There are special materials available for transferring your pattern onto tinware for tole painting. The easiest to find is a type of chalk that is brushed away with one brush stroke. You should consult your art store about these materials.

For liquid embroidery the classic method of transferring is by use of dressmaker's carbon. This special carbon will not damage your fabric and will wash away on the first cleaning. You may also wish to try the new transfer inks called Transpaints, discussed under Canvas Work and Needlepoint. You will find these useful for making your own transfer, even if you wish only line work in one color.

THE STENCIL ARTS

The stencil arts include silk screening, woodblock printing, linoleum printing, floor stenciling, and textile stencils.

Essentially, for all of these techniques you must cut a separate stencil or printing block for each color desired in the finished work. The order in which you select your colors for printing and the techniques you develop in these art forms will determine to a large extent what the finished piece will look like.

To help with registration problems, which are basic to all these techniques, you should redraw each color separately and in sequence on the same-size graph (10-squares-to-the-inch) as used in this book. You will then be able to reassemble your stencils easily and adjust them where necessary without losing registration. When you have determined the exact outlines for each color, you will find it useful to draw your final stencils on clear or mat-finished acetate. Cut through these prior to making your final stencil. You can "test run" the acetate stencils, readjust the patterns, and see clearly where the problems will arise in your printing. I use mat acetate for my final stencils for silk screening, floor stencils, and textile printing with a brush technique. It is very useful to be able to see clearly through to the final work.

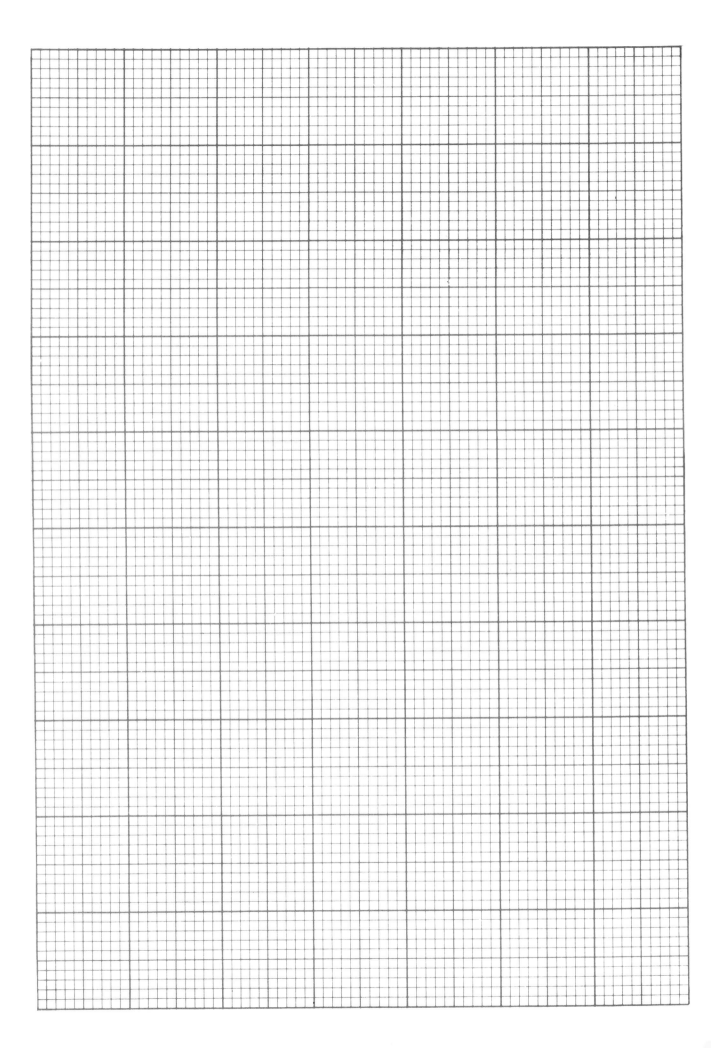

CHAPTER 4:

Texture in Embroidery

Embroidery requires a developed sense of both color and texture. It is indeed a three-dimensional artform and your choice of stitches is as important to the end work as your sense of color. Both contribute to texture.

In this section I have selected several patterns and redrawn them to show the needlecraft stitches as they would look in the finished piece. Notice how clearly the texture stands out when the illustrations are in black-and-white. I have tried to represent traditional, classic approaches in some patterns and a far less traditional selection of stitches in others. Really, there are no rules and you will develop your own vocabulary of stitches that reflect your own style. The end result will be a totally unique work.

The stitches illustrated in this section are detailed in the Glossary of Stitches. A very good reference on texture is *The Art of Crewel Embroidery* by Mildred Davis.

Pattern 1. Traditional Rose

The traditional rose, a popular theme for needlework and the decorative arts, comes in a vast variety of colors and values within the ranges of maroon, red, orange, yellow, pink, and white. The leaves vary in color from deep hunter green to pale olive, and into the brown and red tones. This pattern can be modified by using four roses from either diagonal or by taking the bottom or top four as a single theme. The center cluster of three roses makes a nice small composition.

14. The roses in Pattern 1 are worked in blocked satin and buttonhole stitches; the edges of each petal are done in stem or crewel stitch; the leaves are worked from the center line of the leaf out to the edges in heavy chain stitch; and the stems of the roses are chain stitched. Notice the difference in texture between this drawing and Fig. 15.

15. The roses in Pattern 1 are worked here entirely in long and short stitch and the edges of each petal are outlined in stem or crewel stitch. A few of the petals are worked in satin stitch to give a bit of accent. The leaves are completely in crewel stitch running from the center line out to the tip of each leaf. The stems are in stem or crewel stitch.

Pattern 2. Violet & Lily of the Valley

The pale violet and lily of the valley are popular spring themes. Violets can be cream colored with slightly lavender thread lines or pale violet with darker lavender lines. The leaves are usually a rich green and the very center of the flower is almost always a bright yellow dot. The lily of the valley are off-white—either cream colored or grayed. Their leaves are a rich dark green.

16. The stitching here of Pattern 2 is unconventional for the theme. It is reminiscent of the bulkier threads used in commercial kits. The following stitches have been used: cable chain stitch to outline the leaves of the lily of the valley, running stitch and satin stitch to catch details and fill in the lily of the valley petals. Seeding details the center of the flower and Portuguese stem stitch is used on the leaf stems of the violets and the center stems of the lily of the valley leaves. The feather stitch fills the small leaves of the violet; long and short stitches are used on the petals; crewel stitch is used to outline the stems of all the flowers, and the fishbone catches the tiny leaves of the violet.

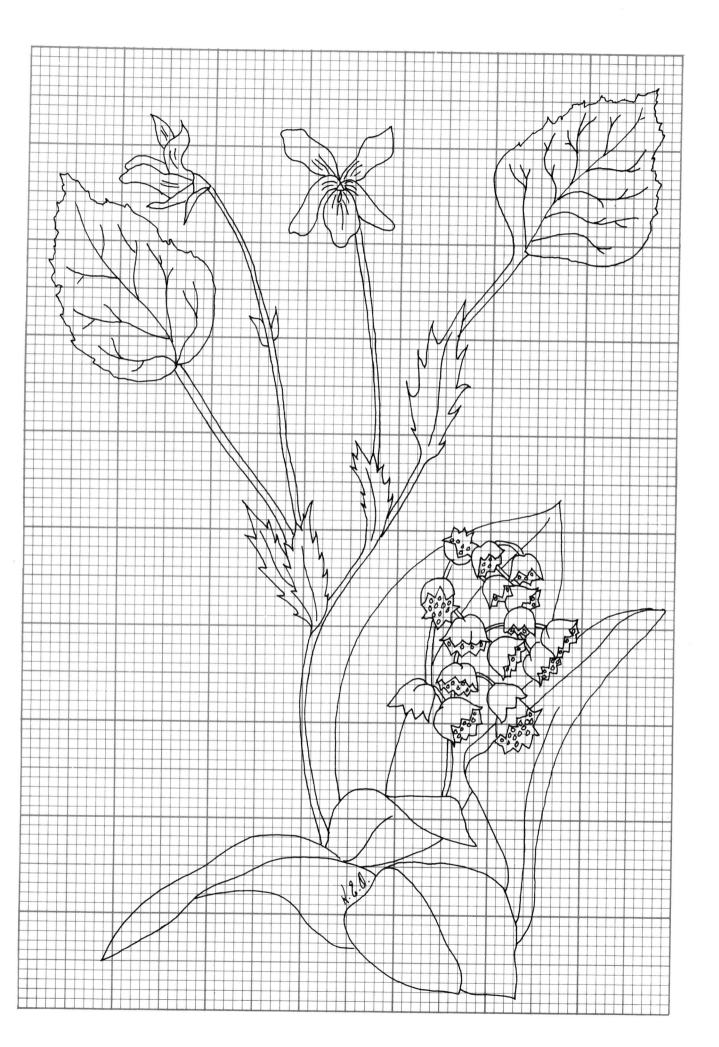

Pattern 3. Geranium

The geranium is probably the most popular potted, summertime plant in the United States. Colors range from vivid magentas and reds to pale pinks and whites with touches of green. The foliage is rich in both texture and of green color, and is sometimes variegated with rust or red-brown tones.

17. The petals of this detailed stitch drawing show the use of bullion knots and fishbone stitch interspersed for texture. The stems are in Portuguese stem stitch for its high texture and the leaves are outlined in the long and short buttonhole stitch. The detailed veining is done in crewel stitch with a tiny French knot at the center.

   You do not need to overcomplicate your stitch selections to have a highly textured and effective piece that can be completed quickly.

Pattern 4. Forsythia

The brilliant yellow forsythia bush is among the very first flowering shrubs of spring and is quickly cut and brought inside for bouquets that cascade with color. The stems are quite woody and often brown in contrast to the flowers.

18. The Portuguese stem stitch is used extensively throughout the twiggy stems with occasional use of straight stitches to break up the line or fill it in. The woody knot in the center stem is filled with French knots. The petals of the flowers are a scattering of Roumanian stitches, split satin stitch, fishbone stitch, and flat stitch. At the center of the flowers are French knots. The detached chain stitch or lazy daisy is used for accent here and there. Padded satin stitches are used on some of the petals.

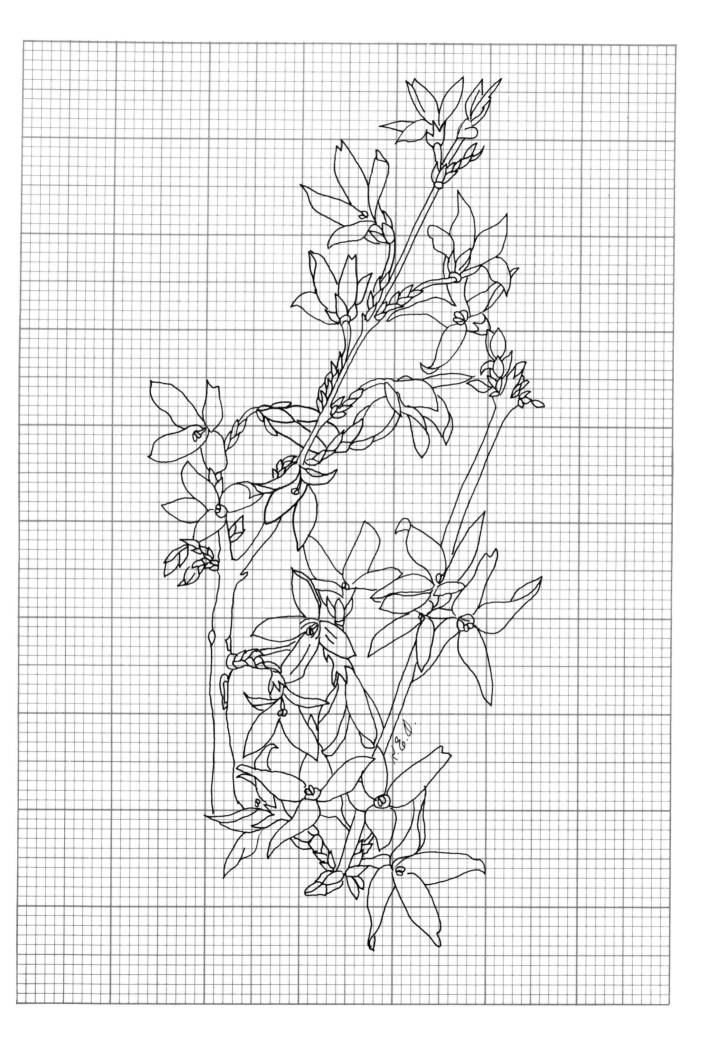

Pattern 5. Cow Pasture Rose

This summer spray is comprised of cow pasture roses, small wild asters, and a touch of perhaps forsythia. Pinks and yellows predominate with the asters perhaps a pale lavender. The center of the pink cow pasture rose is yellow.

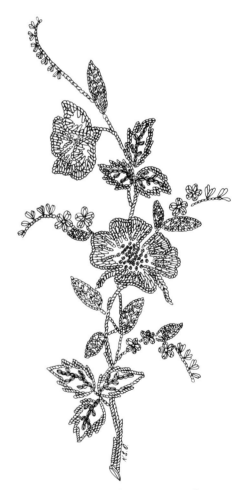

19. The roses are done in long and short stitch with French knots at the center. The edge of the petal on the lower rose is satin stitch. The stems of the forsythia and the bottom rose's stem are in crewel stitch. Coral stitch is used for the smaller stems. The forsythia is represented by lazy daisy stitches and the small leaves of the forsythia are in flat stitch. The leaves of the rose are cretan stitch and the center line is overstitched in a back stitch. Each thorn is a single stitch. The tiny asters are stitched in groups of three satin stitches—two short on each edge with the center stitch of the petal long.

20. Here is a more open look for Pattern 5. The roses are in long and short buttonhole and a second row of crewel stitch is added to the lower petal of the bottom rose. The center of the flower is filled with seeding stitch on the top rose, the other has French knots. The stems of the forsythia are in split stitch throughout and those of the roses are in crewel stitches. The asters are in lazy daisy and the small leaves are double rows of feather stitch outlined in crewel or stem stitches. Two satin stitches per petal give the effect of forsythia buds. Finally the large leaves at the base and those just below the top rose are outlined in stem stitch and filled with tiny chain stitches.

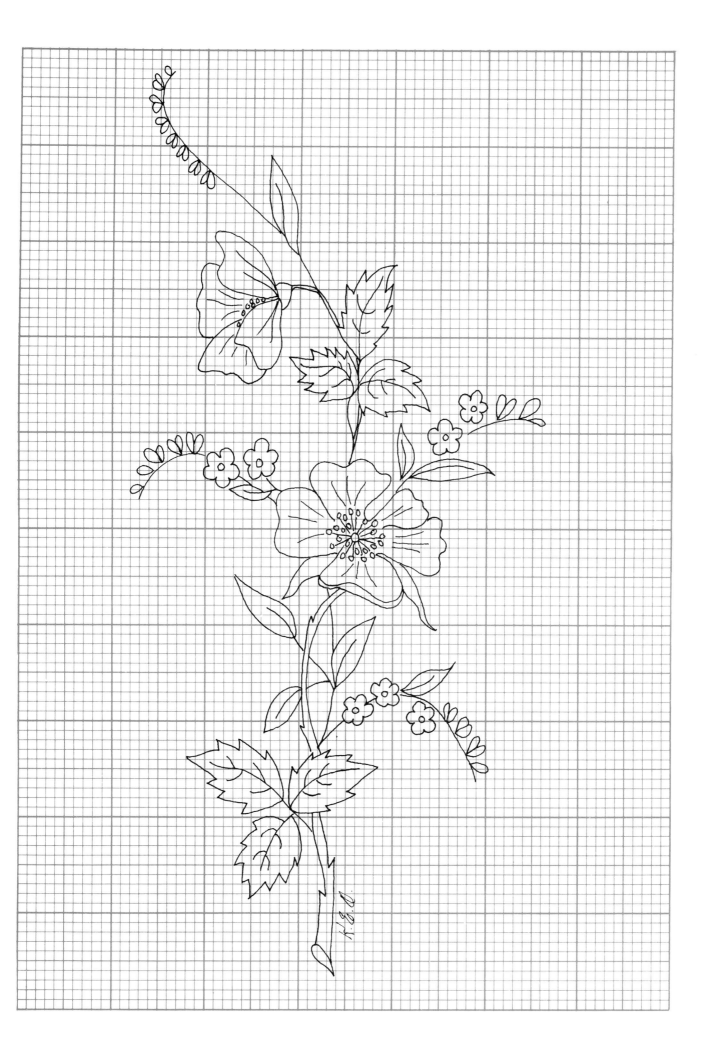

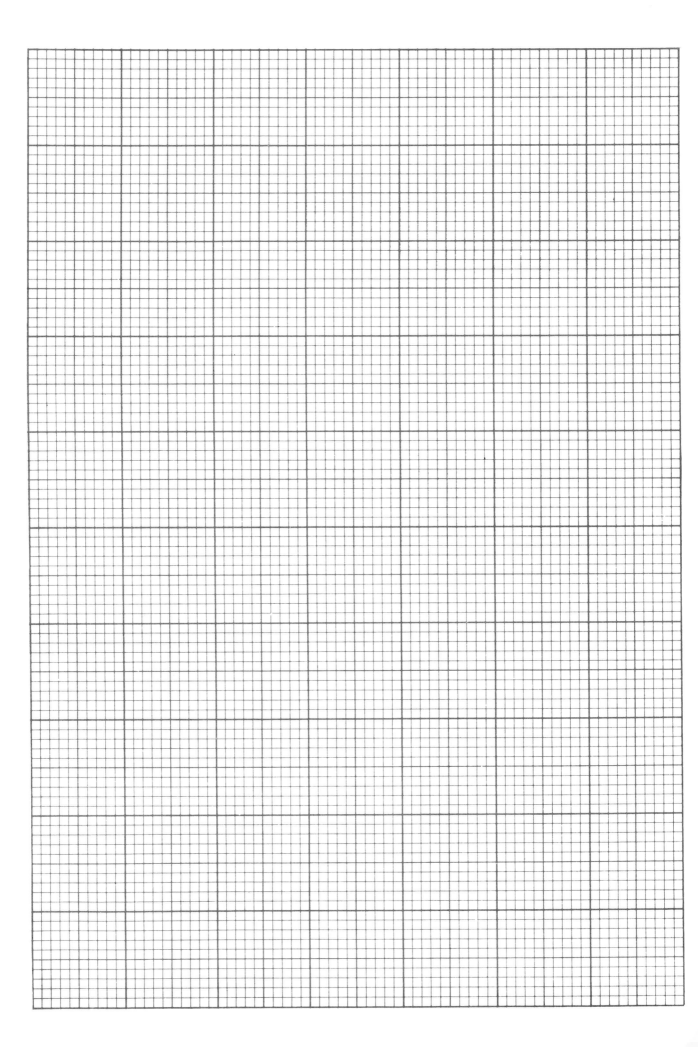

CHAPTER 5:

Patterns from Author's Notebooks

Patterns 1 through 39 originated with my old notebook drawings and seed catalogs over the past years and comprise a library of plants that I have grown or observed personally. Any suggestions on coloring are purely personal and to be ignored by those of you with adventure in your blood. Refer to the resource books in the Bibliography for other coloring suggestions.

Throughout the remaining selection of patterns, there are no detailed stitch drawings. Instead, each pattern is reproduced in two different sizes to extend their usefulness for both large and small projects.

The circles added around Patterns 6 through 11 are to show you one way to frame a design: either work the area outside the circle in a different color or in stitching to complement the florals.

Pattern 6. African Violet

African violets appeal to the green thumb in all plant lovers. They have a wide variety of textures and colors although the illustration here is of the single petal flower.

Colors range from violet, blue, pink, and magenta, to white and even slightly brown tones of red. The leaves can be deep hunter green with a reddish toned underleaf to a pale olive. The center of each flower has tiny yellow seeds.

The leaves are slightly wooly and can be quite stiff. The stems are usually fleshy in texture and snap off easily if twisted slightly. The flower stems are quite stiff and the flowers perk up above the leaves at odd angles.

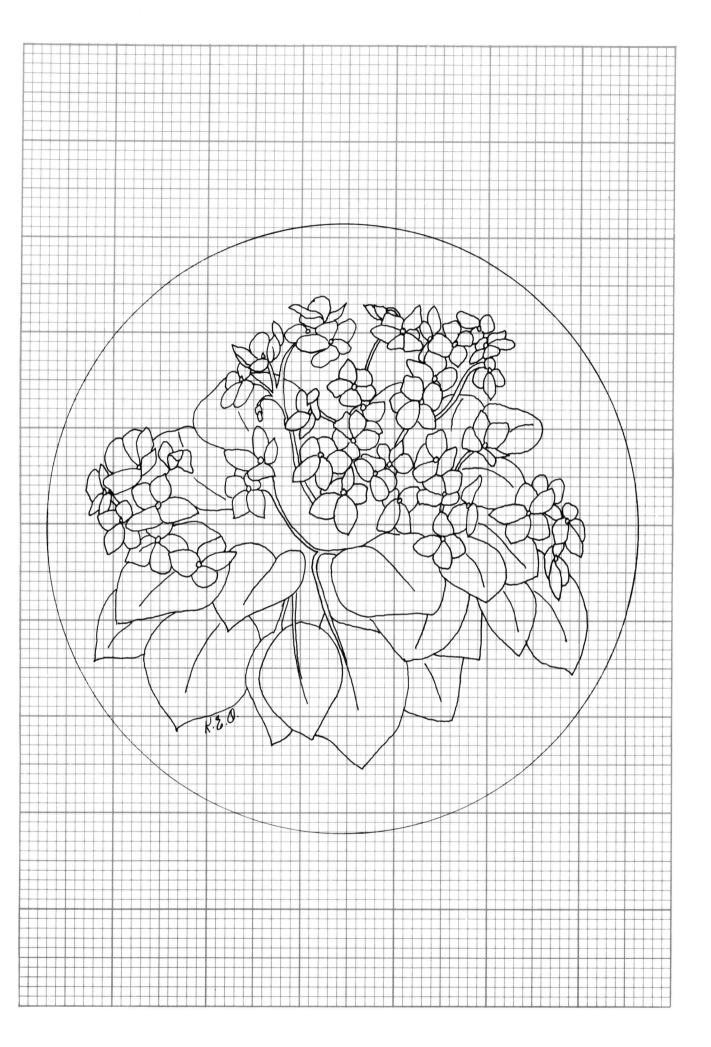

Pattern 7. Blackberry

If you enjoy berry picking in the summer, blackberries are abundant in New Hampshire during the late part of July and early August. Flowers appear on the bushes, which are often referred to as thickets, during late June.

The flowers are the palest tones of cream with the palest pink highlights. At the center of each flower is an abundance of pale yellow pollen. The centermost part of the flower is deeper yellow. The leaves are a rich, yellowish green with touches of red on the dying leaves. The center veins are quite pronounced.

The flower is velvety soft but the buds are quite stiff and hard. The stems are woody and break easily when weighed down by berries. They are very thorny and prickle and grasp your clothing when you get too close.

Pattern 8. Violet & Lily of the Valley

Quite different in effect from Pattern 2, this bouquet of lily of the valley and violets is more compact and less stylistic. The color ranges are similar to those described in Pattern 2; however, these flowers are botanically the common wild violets found throughout the countryside in blues and lavenders. There are some small buttercups poking out around the lily of the valley when you look closely.

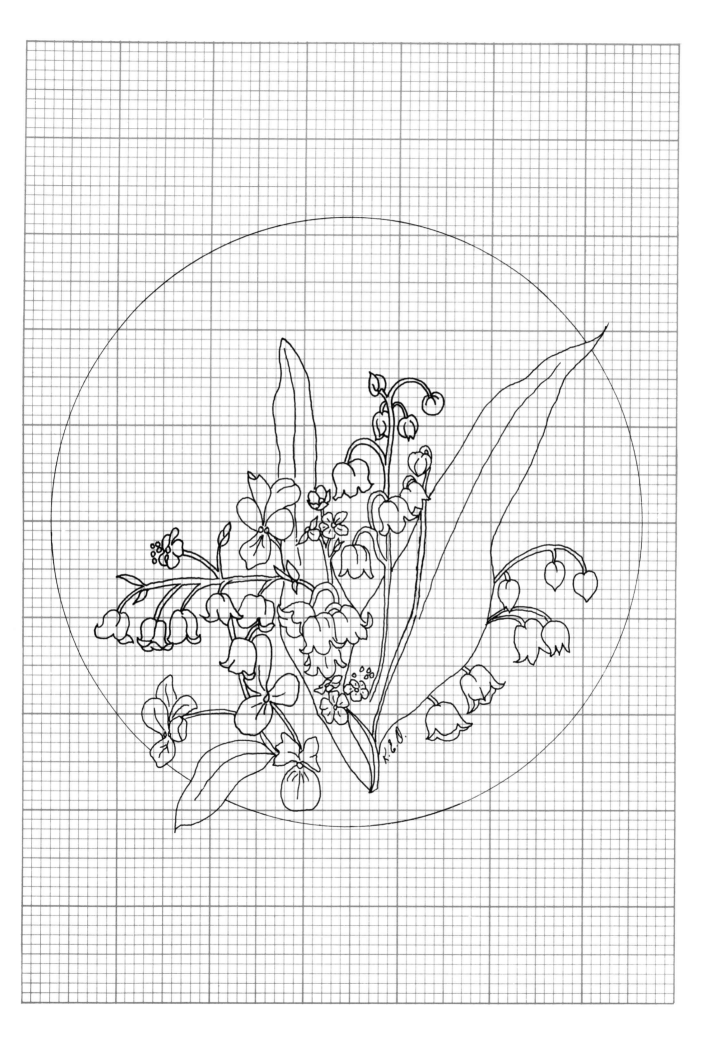

Pattern 9. Peonies

Peonies appear often in ancient Chinese and Japanese designs. They have an elegance all their own. They grow into very large shrubs over twenty years, give off a sweet smelling perfume, and make spectacular bouquets in June when they are in full bloom.

The heavy blossoms bend down the edges of the stalks often to the ground and honey-loving ants abound all over the blooms. The coloring ranges from pure white with small flecks of pink or yellow to pinks and into a very deep red. The foliage is darker tones of green, that give a significant contrast to the blooms.

There are many varieties of peonies. These come from my mother's garden in Wellesley Hills, Massachusetts. Her bushes were well over twenty years old and in pink and white with pink flecks.

Pattern 10. Arum Lily

The arum lily is grown outdoors in milder climates and adds a majesty to any garden. The plant is quite stiff in texture and very exotic in appearance.

The smooth blooms are pale cream to a cream yellow; the leathery leaves, which have a rippled effect, are deep green with highlighted center veins. The stalks of the flowers are pale, almost yellow-green in contrast to the foliage.

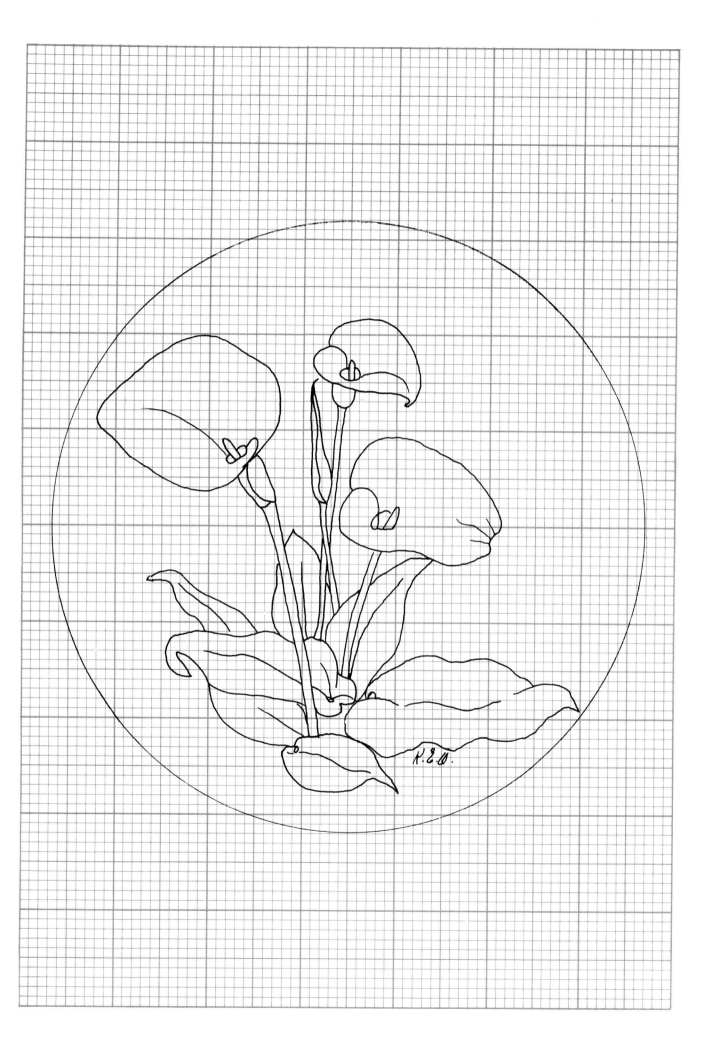

Pattern 11. Fuchsia

Fuchsia is a very popular hanging-basket plant. It is colorful and produces an enormous abundance of flowers all summer long.

The leaves are small and dark green in all varieties. The flowers, however, give you a wide variety of color combinations. Some varieties are all one color: violet-blue, red, and pure white. Those which are two colors always have one color on the outer petals and the other on the "sepals" which look like the inner skirt to a dancer's costume.

Bicolor blooms are purple with pink sepals, blue with white sepals, rose red with white sepals, soft pink with white sepals, and white with red sepals. The colors are usually quite vivid although my own plant was soft pink with white sepals.

The blooms are surprisingly stiff. The stems are thin and quite fragile and bend easily from the weight of the flowers. The foliage is soft to the touch and visibly veined.

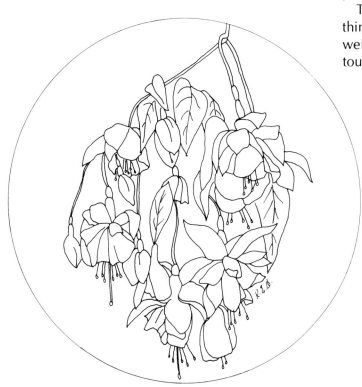

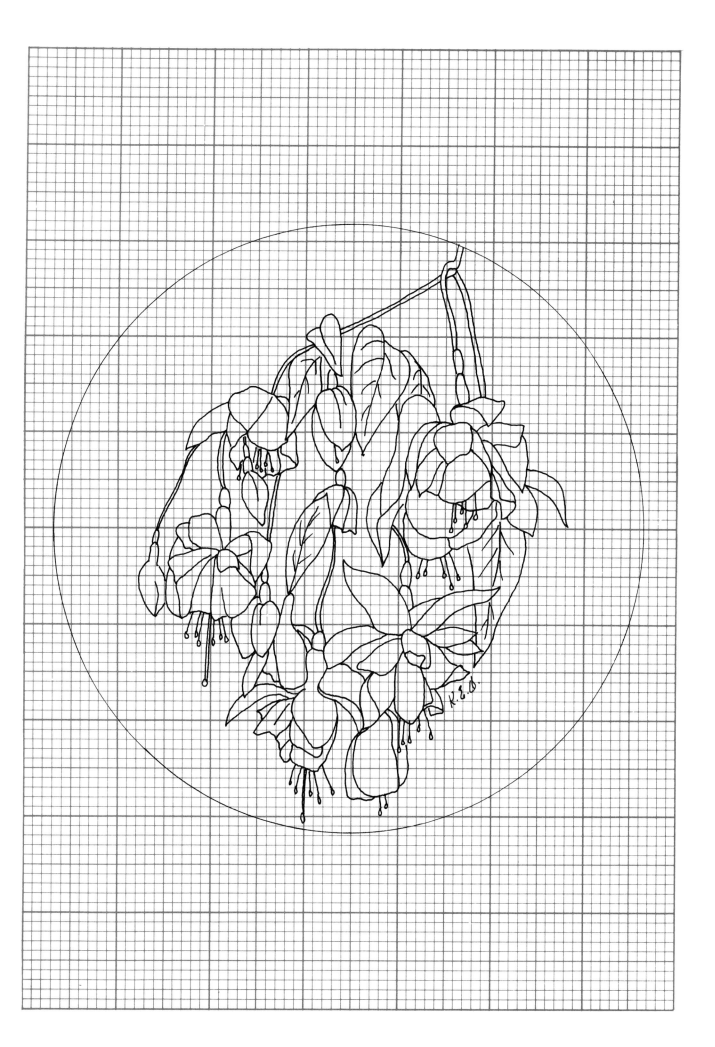

Pattern 12. Lily of the Valley #1

Lily of the valley are always white or the palest cream. Their foliage is dark green and the stems are usually quite stiff and lighter green bordering on yellow-green.

The petals of the flower are highly textured and you will find the use of various stitches both suitable and effective.

The left section of this pattern was flopped and used at the base of the violet in Pattern 2. This is only one way in which you can use sections of patterns as part of another work of your own creation.

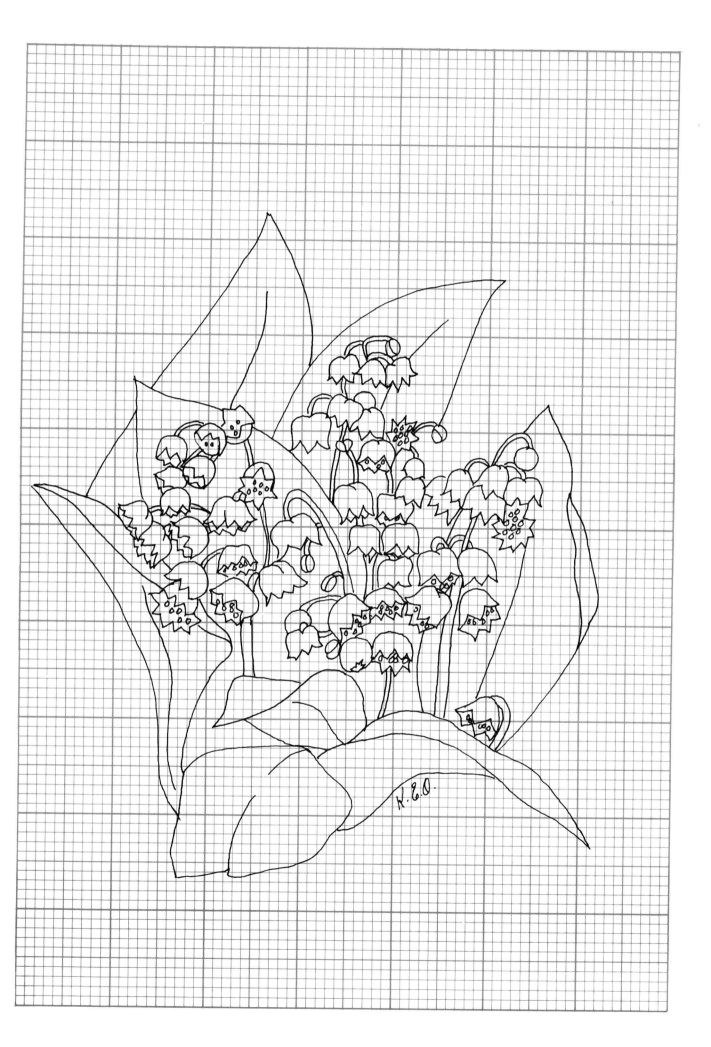

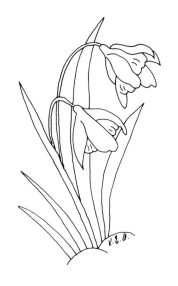

Pattern 13. Snowdrop

The pure white snowdrop blossoms are quite heavy causing them to droop. The foliage is stiff and perky like crocuses. The inner sepals are often touched with a contrasting green-brown color toward the edges. The petals and leaves are very smooth in texture. Snowdrops bloom in late winter and early spring like the crocus. This pattern was used to illustrate counted thread work in Chapter 3.

Pattern 14. Primrose

This pattern was used to illustrate counted thread work in Chapter 3.

The Primrose is found in rock gardens throughout the United States and all over Europe and the Middle East. The colors vary widely with each variety but pale yellow, pale lavender, and pink are common. The foliage is very textured and somewhat wooly like the African violet. Again, the coloring varies but gray-greens and pale yellow-green veining is suitable.

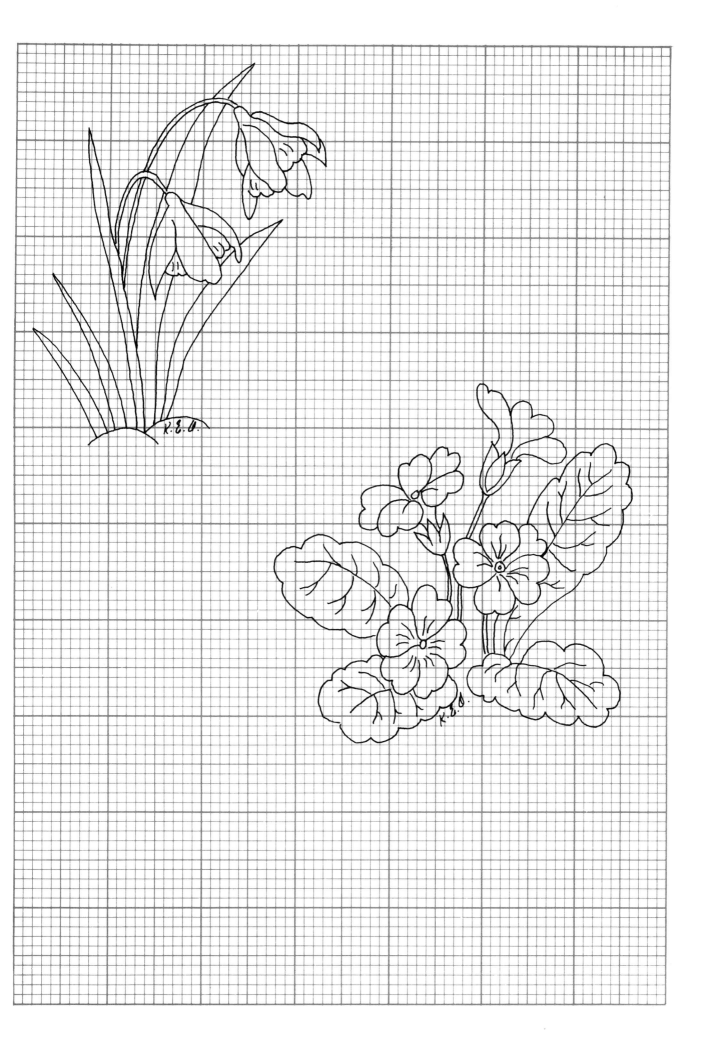

Pattern 15. Cherry Blossom

The traditional cherry blossom heralds spring in our nation's capitol, Washington, D.C. The blooms are pale pink and white with yellow pollen at the center of each. The stem of the branch is woody in texture and brown in color. When young, the leaves are light green on the yellowish side. You could select almost any type of stitch combinations and have an interesting spray of blooms.

Pattern 16. Dogwood Bloom

The dogwood bloom appears around the countryside at about the same time as the cherry blossom. They are either pink or white in color. The center seeds are very green with a contrasting touch of yellow. The limbs are quite woody and can tend toward the red tones although the texture is not as rough as the cherry tree. The leaves are deep in color and can have almost a blue tone.

50

Pattern 17. Moccasin Flower

The moccasin flower, a wild flower common to New Hampshire, is related to the lady slipper but has an earthier look in coloring with a deep pouch of bloom in rich pink. The oval-shaped leaves at the back of the pouch are a rich light brown and the outer leaves, stem, and lower leaves are green. The entire flower is heavily textured and veined.

Pattern 18. Sweet Peas

The sweet pea trails over gardens in summer. The blooms are palest pastels to deep rich reds and include yellows, lavenders, pinks, oranges, and white. The stalks are quite stiff although the flowers are very light and airy. The leaves are lighter tones of green.

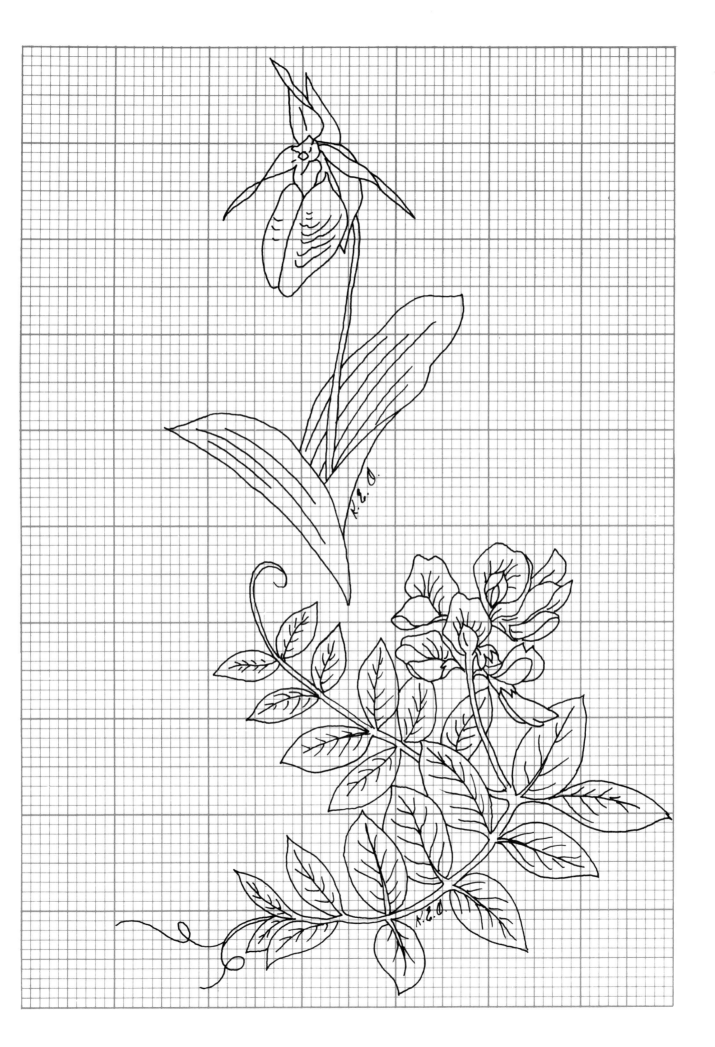

Pattern 19. Rose Bud

The traditional rose bud design has been used in needlework throughout the centuries. It is possible to combine this pattern with the other traditional rose patterns and have them look stylistically correct. Any coloring found in the rose family is suitable and the foliage can include red tones which are common to a number of varieties in their new growth. The stems are thorny.

Pattern 20. Petunias

This pattern captures only a few petunia blooms out of what is usually a spectacular display in summer gardens. There are so many colors available that almost anything will look right. Many varieties are variegated and veined if multicolored blooms suit your taste. The foliage is usually slightly fuzzy.

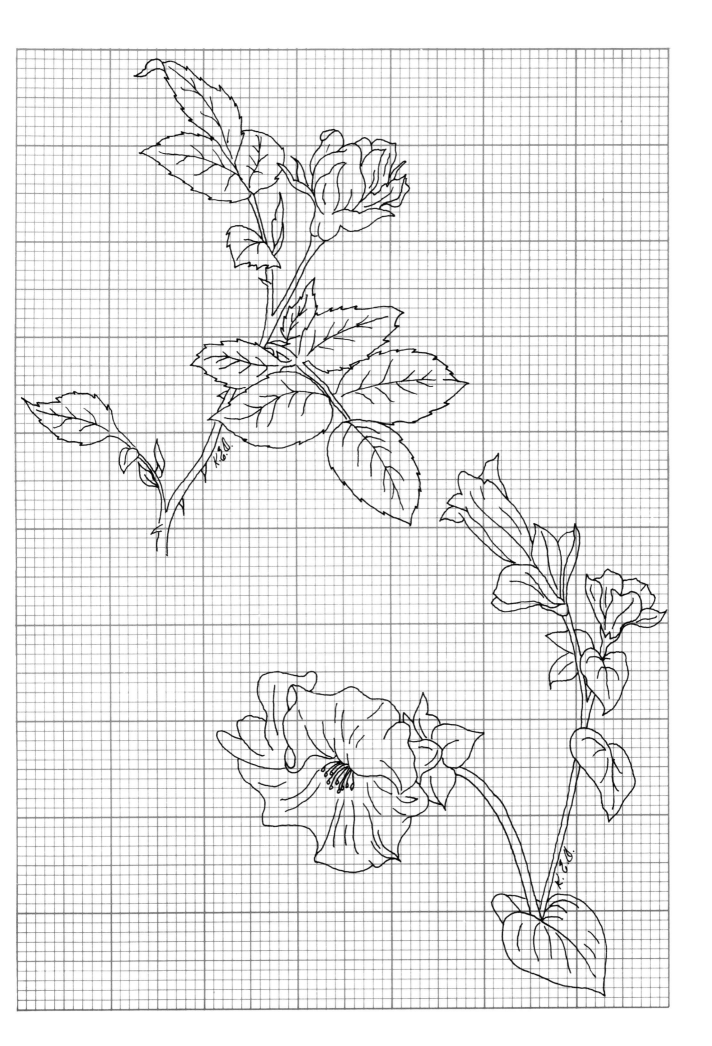

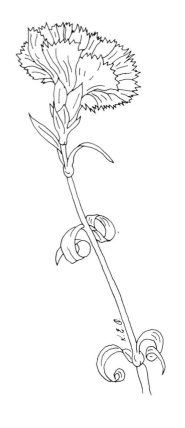

Pattern 21. Carnation #1

The coloring of this single carnation stem and bloom can vary from pure white to deep rich red. Its fragrance is heavenly. The deep green stalk and leaves are stiff but smooth to the touch. The petals of the bloom appear so full when seen from the front that they appear stiff although they are velvety and soft individually.

Pattern 22. Bachelor Button

Also known as the cornflower, this bloom abounds in the wild around the country. The plant can be quite bushy and packed with rather stiff flowers of white, pink, and the traditional "cornflower" blue. The foliage is deep green tending toward blue tones. This is a good pattern for texture stitches.

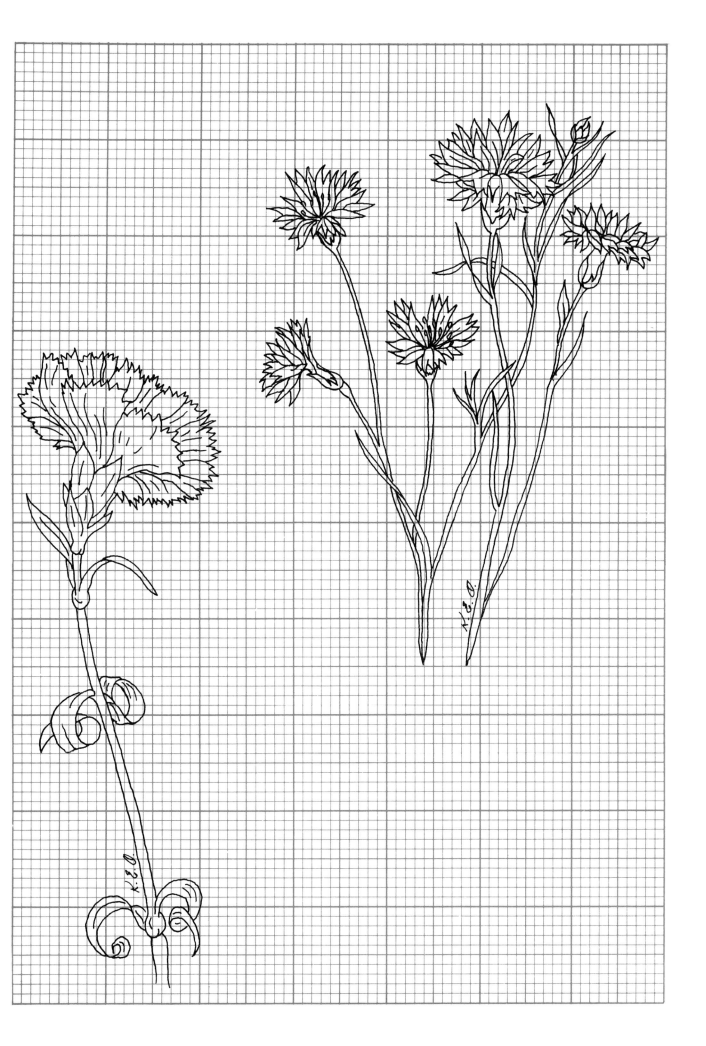

Pattern 23. Chrysanthemum

The varieties of this flower, presented here as simplified as possible, are many and very traditional to Oriental artists. The "incurved" type of blossom is shown here. Its colors are primarily yellow, white, brown, pink, or red. The foliage is usually a very deep and rich, blue-toned green.

This is a particularly good pattern to use different types of textured stitches for each flower petal. Begin with the petals at the back of the flower and work toward the front petals.

The blooms are often so heavy that they bend the more fragile stems but most plants will grow a stiff stalk if properly fertilized.

Pattern 24. Fringed Gentian

This wildflower likes the open meadows of the countryside. It grows as an annual and changes its location from year to year. It flowers from fall until frost.

The edges of the dark blue petals are quite fringed and airy. The trumpet shape of the flower gives it a sturdy effect. The foliage is a medium green.

This pattern is most suitable in combination with the Walcott Watercolor patterns presented later in Chapter 7.

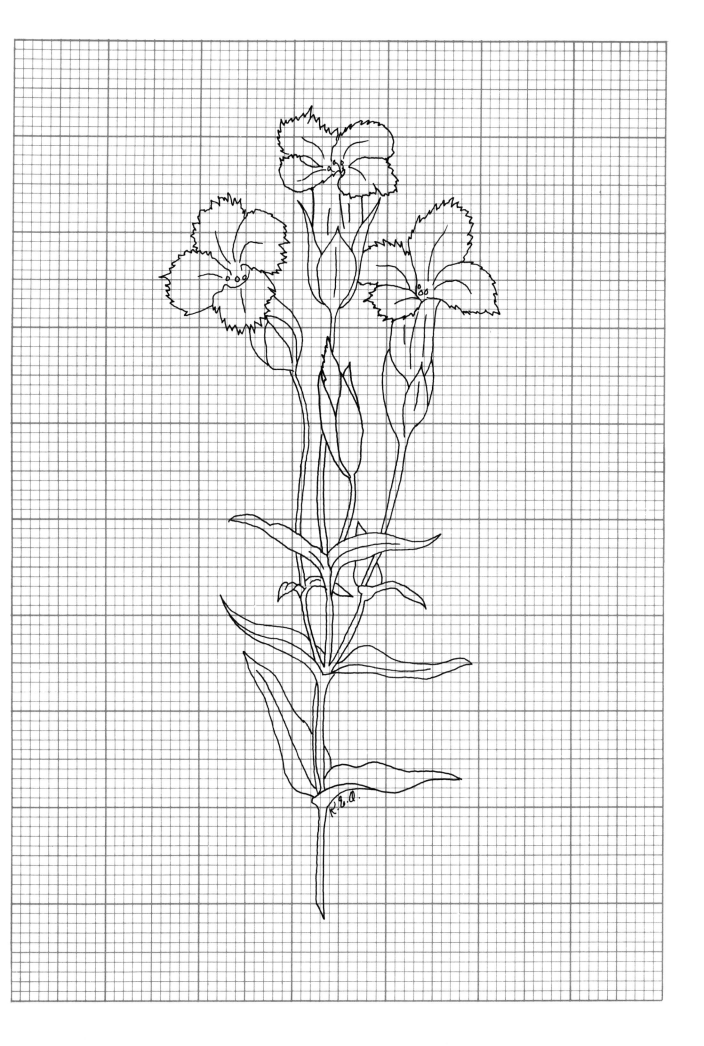

Pattern 25. Rough-fruited Cinquefoil

A relative of the rose family, this flower is found growing wild along the roads in New Hampshire and tucked away along the edges of the woods. It is rather hairy in texture and more leafy than this slightly abstracted version shows. The flowers are pale yellow and the foliage, a rich contrasting green.

You can add seeding to the center areas of each bloom with tiny French knots. The stalks are quite stiff and hold the cluster of flowers high and proudly.

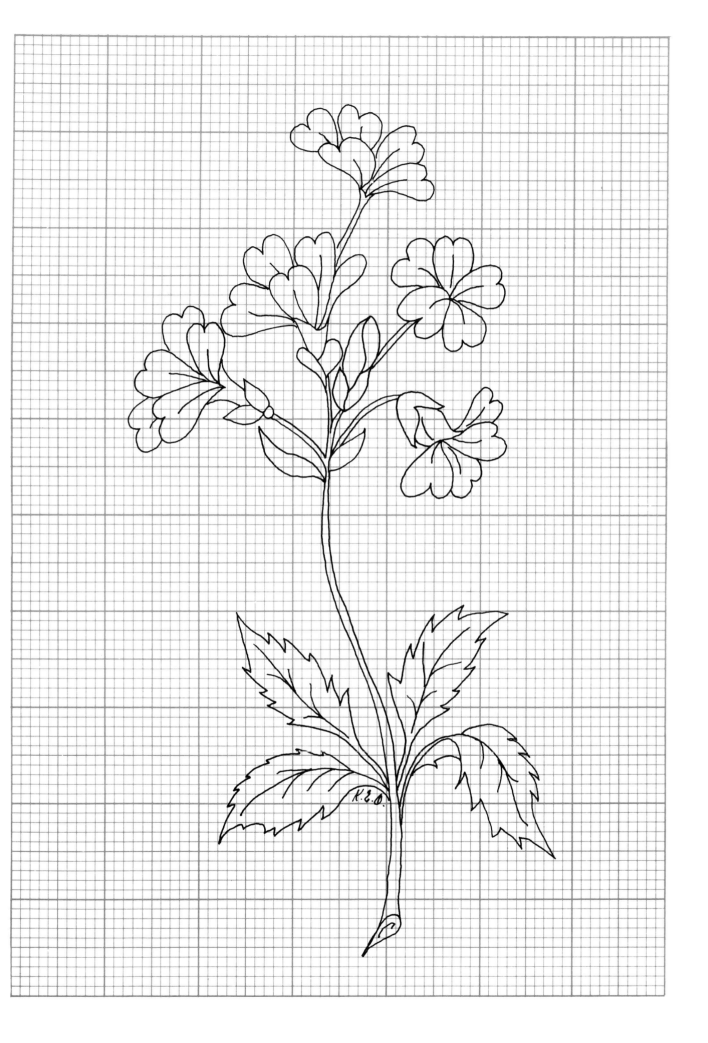

Pattern 26. Tulip #1

The tulip bulb is a spring favorite all over the world. The color range now includes almost every color in the spectrum from red through violet.

Tulip blossoms are firm and smooth. The flowers are usually very erect but occasionally heavy enough to bend the stem slightly. The stem coloring is a rich, and often quite deep green.

Many varieties are multicolored so you can let your own taste prevail for a very dramatic work. This pattern takes a cluster of three blossoms and then flops them over without the center flower to make the bottom two. This is one way to develop a composition of flowers for a project.

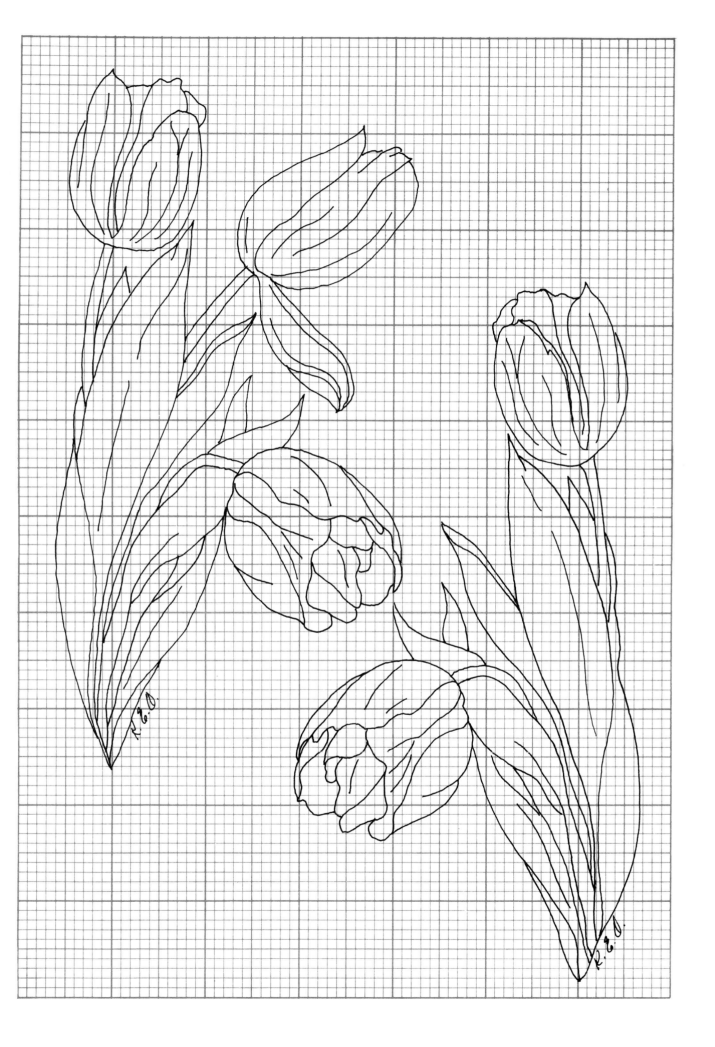

Pattern 27. Jonquil

The yellow jonquil belongs to the narcissus family. It is distinguished by rounded leaves and a slightly pink-yellow center cup contrasting with petals of pure buttercup yellow.

The leaves, which are quite stiff and thin, are a very deep green tending toward yellow.

The outer petals are quite smooth with distinct grooves toward the center. The inner cup is somewhat shorter than the daffodil's and very rippled in texture. The leaves are rather like reeds and smooth with a slight browning toward the tip of the leaf where it dies back.

There is no reason to restrict your coloring to that of the traditional flower. Narcissus can have white outer leaves with yellow inner cups tipped with orange-red to bright red inner cups highlighted with brilliant yellow pollen. They are sometimes all white or all yellow with slightly darker inner cups.

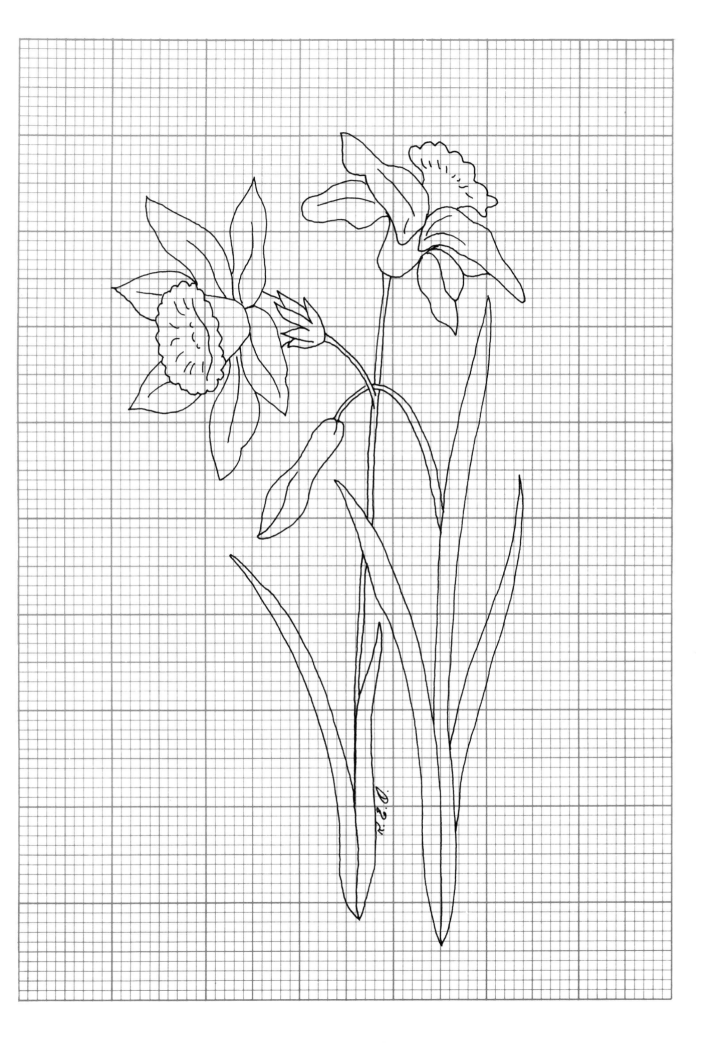

Pattern 28. Daffodil #1

Daffodils are easily recognized by large inner cups surrounded by full outer petals. Like the jonquil, they are traditionally all yellow; however, there are now many new color combinations available.

The leaves are almost always flat and elongated with a very distinct center groove of a darker green. They have a tendency to twist slightly in their long upward growth.

This pattern is abstracted from Pattern 33 which shows only the flowers. You can develop an entirely new pattern by selecting a grouping of flowers and superimposing other blooms with the selection. This is particularly useful when you wish to fit a pattern into a given area such as on placemats, a lamp base, an elongated pillow, or the collar of a particular garment.

Pattern 29. Canterbury Bell

Canterbury bells are popular in English needle-work. The plants are biannuals and grow wild in rocky areas.

The flowers vary from white, pink, and blue to mauve and deep purple and have distinct star-shaped center stamens in pale yellow. There are distinct vein lines of slightly deeper color along the blooms which tend to give a slight thread look to the petals.

The leaves are a soft green against a brown twig-type stem. The stems are many branched and grow to be quite stiff. The outer lip of the flower tends to bend outward.

Pattern 30. Gardenia

This single gardenia is shown in full bloom. The flowering bush, which originated in China, is sometimes called cape jasmine. It gives off an unbelievable sweet, powerful perfume and bruises very easily when touched. The heavily veined leaves are a crisp, shiny, deep emerald green.

The bloom opens with pure white, almost velvet in texture, petals. As it fades, it turns to a cream color and into the softer taupes.

The brown stems are twiggy. Usually the shrub is thickly covered with leaves in quite irregular branching patterns.

Pattern 31. Daisy

For these abstracted daisy blossoms you can select any coloring your heart desires. Generally, the daisy has a fluffy yellow or brown center. The petals can be any color, but only one color per plant. If you want shasta daisies, make the centers yellow—perhaps embroidered in turkey work— and the petals white with a deep, rich hunter green background. For Livingstone (or African) daisies, make the centers bright orange and shade the petals from white in the center to a bright pink at the outside. Another version of daisy has paler tones of orange and pink with rust red-orange centers and no shading on the petals. Of course, the black-eyed and brown-eyed Susans have yellow petals and, like their names imply, black or brown centers. Another variety, called the green-headed coneflower; looks much like the black-eyed Susan except that the center is green and the petals usually angle downward and slightly away from the center.

Pattern 32. Crocus #1

Crocus blooms are illustrated here without their leaves as they appear when poking their heads up through the last of the winter snows.

The color for this cheerful flower ranges from pure white with bright yellow stamen, to yellow and pale to deep violet. The leaves, if you wish to add a few, are long and thin with a white vein running down the center of each. The center of each flower is a brilliant yellow, perhaps worked in a cluster of French knots.

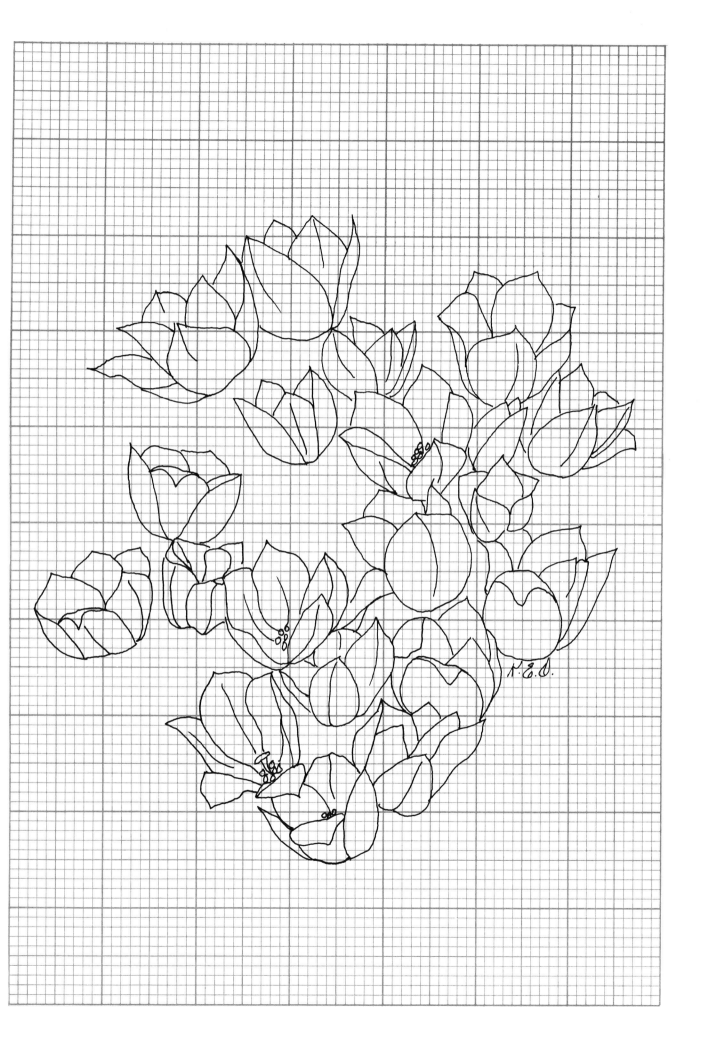

Pattern 33. Daffodil #2

The upper right three flowers from this pattern were used for Pattern 28. See how you can abstract what you want?

The coloring suggestions for Pattern 28 also apply here.

If you wish a smaller arrangement, look at the following combinations which are appropriate for differently shaped spaces: 1, 2, and 5 (Pattern 28); 1, 2, and 3; 3, 4, and 5; 3, 4, and 7; 4, 5, and 7; 4, 5, and 6; and 4, 6, and 7. The variations are infinite. If you want to do a series of placemats with each one slightly different, try these variations. The series will blend well, have the same color combinations, and look as though you carefully designed each one differently. Why not try this in counted thread work?

Pattern 34. Gladiolus

Gladiolus are native to South Africa where many exotic flowers originate. These spectacular and regal blooms grow very tall with a profusion of blossoms. New flowers grow at the top of the stakelike stem; the older blooms fade and drop off from the bottom. The result is continuous bloom for up to six weeks per plant.

The coloring is varied. White, yellow, pink, red, crimson, mauve, and purple flowers are all found and often they are bicolored. The stems are a rich, often slightly blue, green and smooth in texture. The leaves, if you wish to add a few, are tall and narrow.

The center stamens are often white or a lighter version of the flower color.

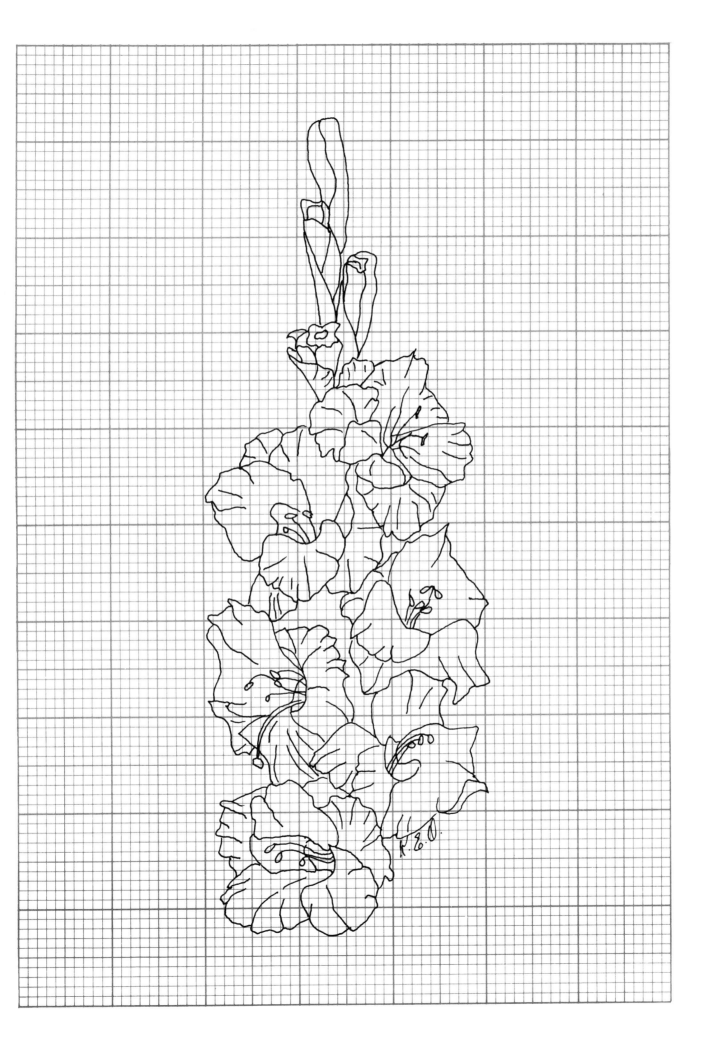

Pattern 35. Turk's Cap Lily

This pattern was drawn from the Turk's cap lily that grows wild in the New Hampshire countryside. However, the pattern can be used for a wide variety of lilies including: goldband lily, speciosum lily, the common lily, as well as the tiger lily.

The Turk's cap lily is deep orange-red with spotting in almost a crimson color with pale pink or white on the back edge of the spots. The stamen are the same burnt red-orange as the petals with the very center in the green of the stem and foliage.

The goldband lily is white with yellow starlike veins from the center and brown-orange spotting. The stamens are deep brown-orange and the very center is the palest green-white. Again the foliage and stems are a deep blue-green.

The speciosum lily is the palest pink with deeper pink veining and the palest green at the very center. The stamens are deep pink; the stems, a very pale green. Foliage is deep green.

The common lily is yellow with crimson spots, crimson stamen, and pale green-yellow stem. The crimson can also border on brown tones. Foliage is deep green.

Tiger lilies are shrimp orange with dark almost brown spots and stamens. The stamen stems are paler shrimp and a chartreuse at the center. Foliage is a deep olive green.

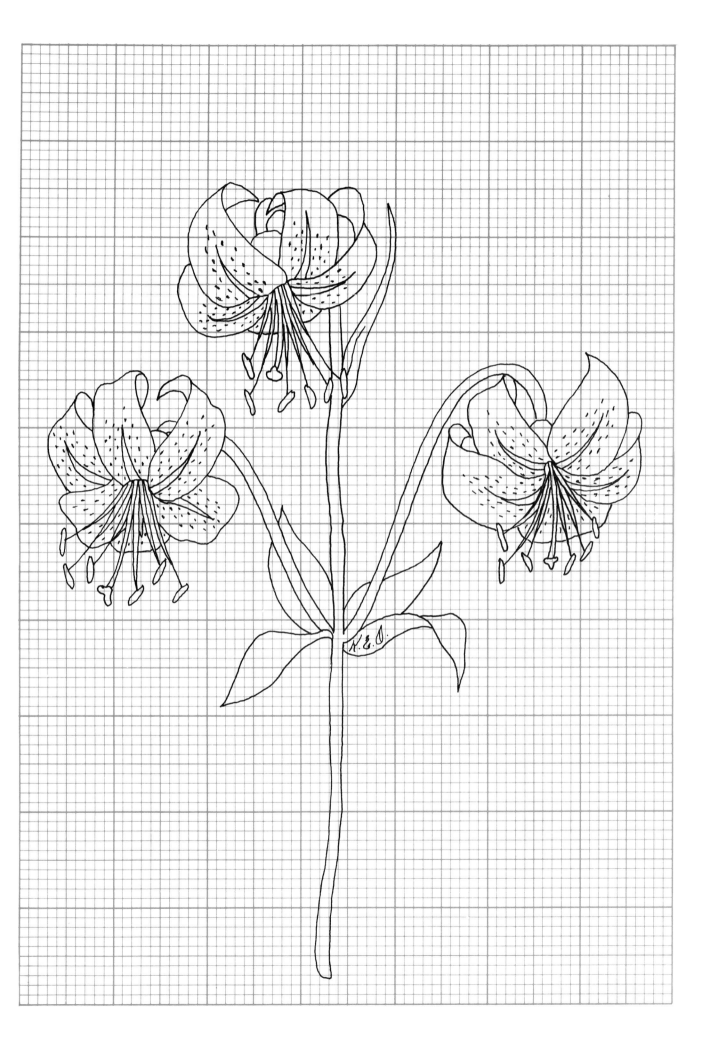

Pattern 36. Day Lily

Day lilies abound in the wilds of New Hampshire where they are usually yellow or orange in color.

This slightly abstracted version allows you to interpret the design as any of the more exotic varieties, including the amaryllis.

Amaryllis come in a wide variety of brilliant and pale colors including the palest taupe with white veining and orange stamen; and a bright red bloom with pale green star-shaped centers, yellow stamen, and a stamen stem that matches the color of the petals.

The belladonna lily is a very pale pink and white with a pale cream yellow stamen, and stamen stem of pale pink.

The bourbon lily is pure white with a bright orange-yellow stamen on a white stem. The foliage is a pale olive which is repeated along the outer edges of the buds.

The regal lily is reddish orange on the outside of the buds with outer petals in streaks of yellow-green. The inner flower is bright yellow at the center becoming quite pale at the outer edge. The stamens are a brilliant yellow-orange on a pale yellow-green stamen stem. The foliage is almost emerald green.

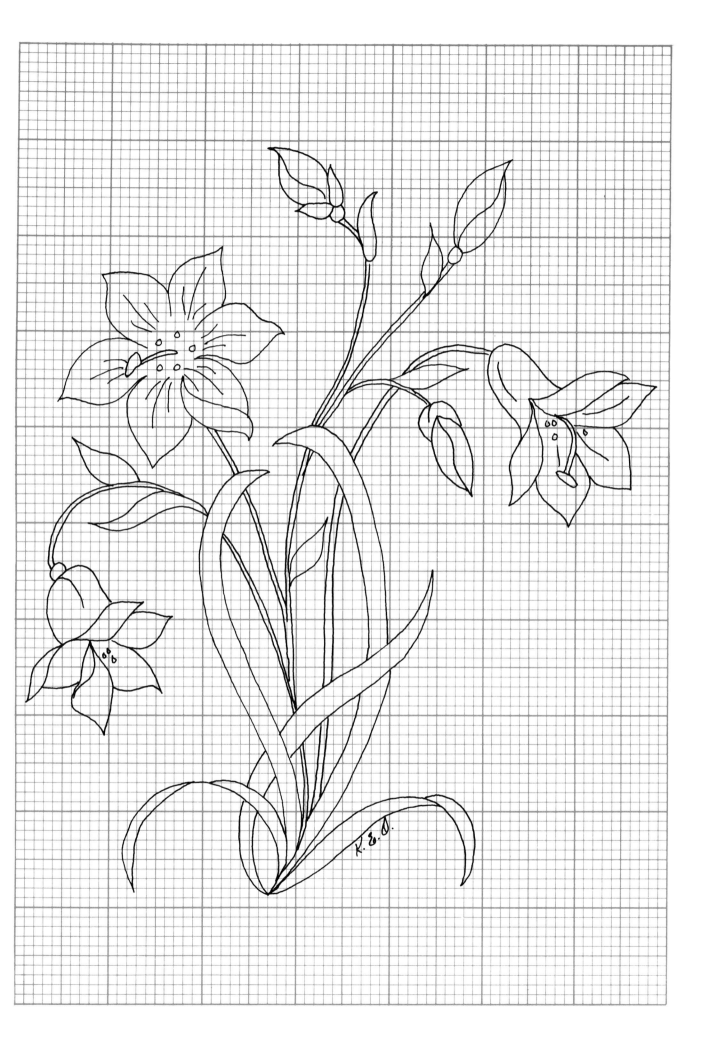

Pattern 37. Tulip #2

Tulips have been a very special subject in embroidery since the Jacobean and Elizabethan periods when they became such a scarce commodity that family fortunes were made and lost in commodities speculation.

These blossoms are abstracted. For different tulip shapes and foliage refer back to Pattern 26. Again, as with the daffodil pattern, you can group several blossoms to make a series of similar but not identical patterns.

If you want just one tulip blossom, use the one in the lower right of the drawing. With the leaves which fall at the back, front right, and base, this single bloom would be a perfect accent to any small project.

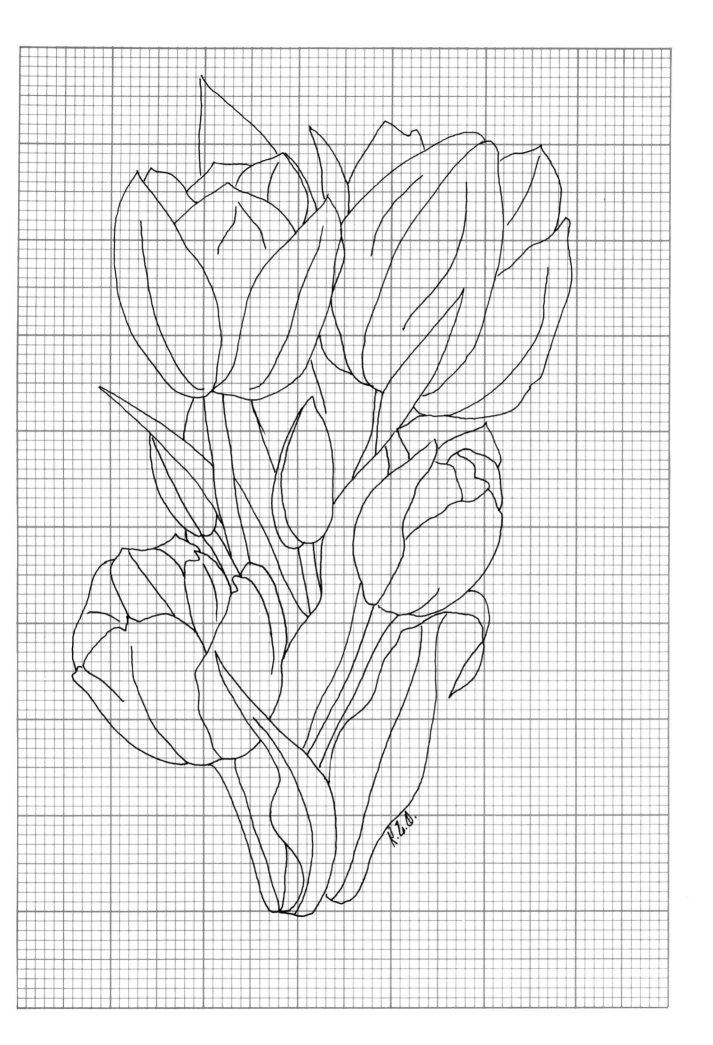

Pattern 38. Iris #1

The flag iris grows wild about the marsh areas of New Hampshire. The outer petals are deep violet; the inner section of petals is white touched with yellow. The veining is deep purple. The inner petals point upward toward the sky and are a pale lavender blue with deep purple center veins. The foliage is a moderately deep tone of yellow-green.

If you see this pattern as the dwarf iris because of the shorter foliage and stems, then increase the yellow area at the center of the lower petals so that only the slightest white edges the area. Add only a few purple veins around this area and eliminate the remaining veins.

If you love yellow, convert this pattern to the yellow iris by making all the petals yellow and following the veining with a pale brown. Keep the veining in only the center of the petal.

Pattern 39. Water Lily

The fragrant water lily is found throughout the eastern United States. From a distance the flowers appear white, but when you get closer, they can be quite pink. The center stamens are bright yellow and the foliage is a deep olive green on top and quite purplish underneath.

The flowers and foliage are quite stiff to the touch; the underneath side of the leaves, heavily veined; and the surface, very smooth and shiny.

If you wish to make this pattern quite exotic, convert the lilies to red water lilies, which are originally from India, by making them the brightest shade of red against an absolutely round, flat, somewhat reddish leaf.

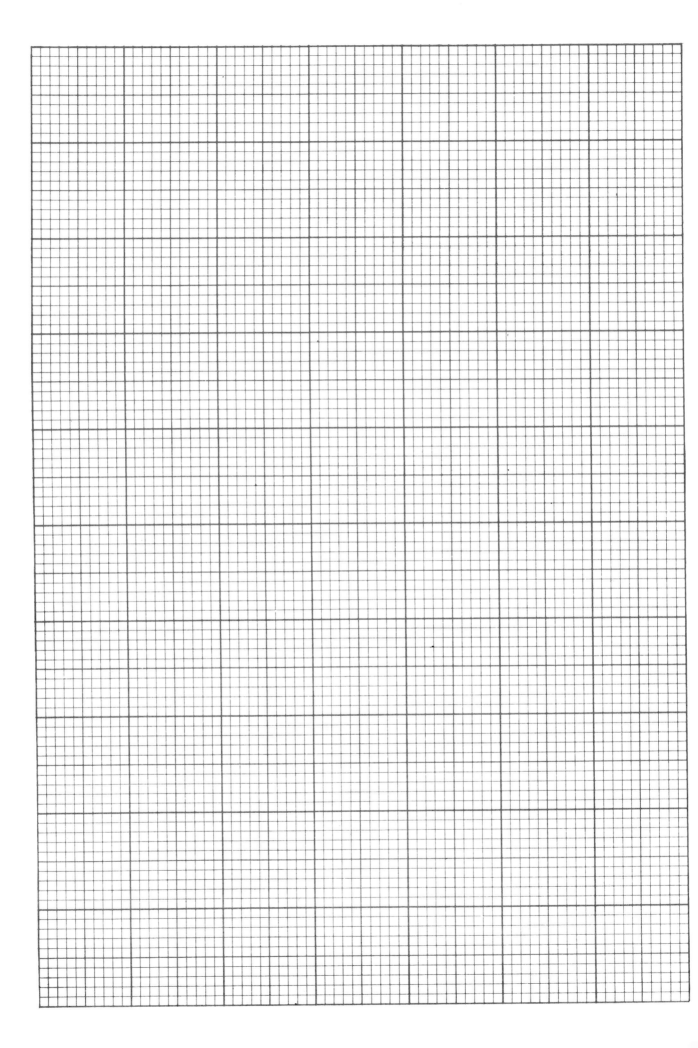

CHAPTER 6:

Mountain Flowers in Color

The patterns that follow are adaptations of the original illustrations by Daphne Barry and Mary Grierson for the English book *Mountain Flowers in Color* by Anthony Huxley. Why I chose this work instead of perhaps the *Field Guide to Wildflowers* by Roger Tory Peterson and Margaret McKenny is hard to define—perhaps it was because the drawings are more stylistically in tune with my own style of drawing. I also like to see the whole plant right down to its root system as it is illustrated in *Mountain Flowers in Color.*

Botanical reference works are a rich source of pattern designs that the craftsman often overlooks when searching for new ideas. You will find their delicate coloring and plant descriptions helpful in your painting and drawing.

I have given the English rather than Latin names for these plants and the *Mountain Flowers in Color* illustration number and text page for reference.

Pattern 40. Marsh Cinquefoil

The marsh cinquefoil is a relative of the rose family. (*Mountain Flowers in Color,* III. 300, text p. 255)

The foliage of these wildflowers is yellow-green with a whitish tone on the underside. They are sometimes rather hairy in texture and are found in wet areas such as swamps and flooded fields.

The blossoms are very distinct in coloring and shape. The outer petals are a deep reddish purple and the inner petals, a slightly lighter tone. The stamens are bright yellow at the tip as is the very center of the bloom. The outside of the petals on just-opening young flowers are touched with a bit of green; the new bud is almost all green with just the slightest touch of purple at its base. The stalk is brownish and rather twiggy.

The common cinquefoil is quite different in shape and yellow in color.

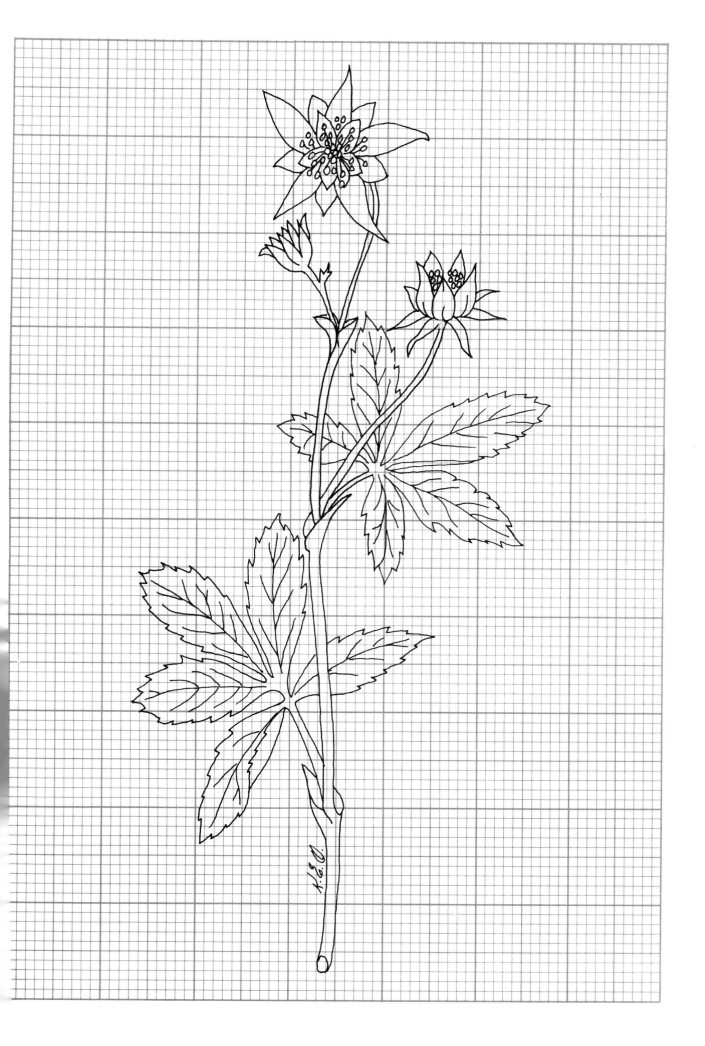

Pattern 41. Superb Pinks

The superb pink is a member of the dianthus family of pinks and is found on the mountainsides at higher elevations. (*Mountain Flowers,* Ill. 100, Text p. 193)

The leaves of this plant grow opposite each other in pairs along a tall and somewhat crisp stalk. The leaves are narrow with a distinct veining up the center of each.

The superb pink is one of the most heavily fringed of the species. The flowers are pink or purplish tending to gray green at the neck and a clear apple green at the "collar" which extends up from the stem.

The stems and leaves are usually quite green but one variety has a rather blue tone.

Pattern 42. Queen of the Alps Thistle

The spectacular queen of the alps thistle is a member of the cow parsley family. (*Mountain Flowers,* Ill. 439, Text p. 295)

This heavily textured bloom is bluish in color with touches of green and purple. The center portion is quite deep and a violet-blue color with white seeds visible in three rows.

The foliage is very spiny and prickly and stiff to the touch. The stems are brown in tone with a slight blue-green overcast and very rigid and stiff.

This is a rare version of thistle and appears in rather rocky soil in open fields in the mountains of Europe. I do not know whether it is found at all in the United States.

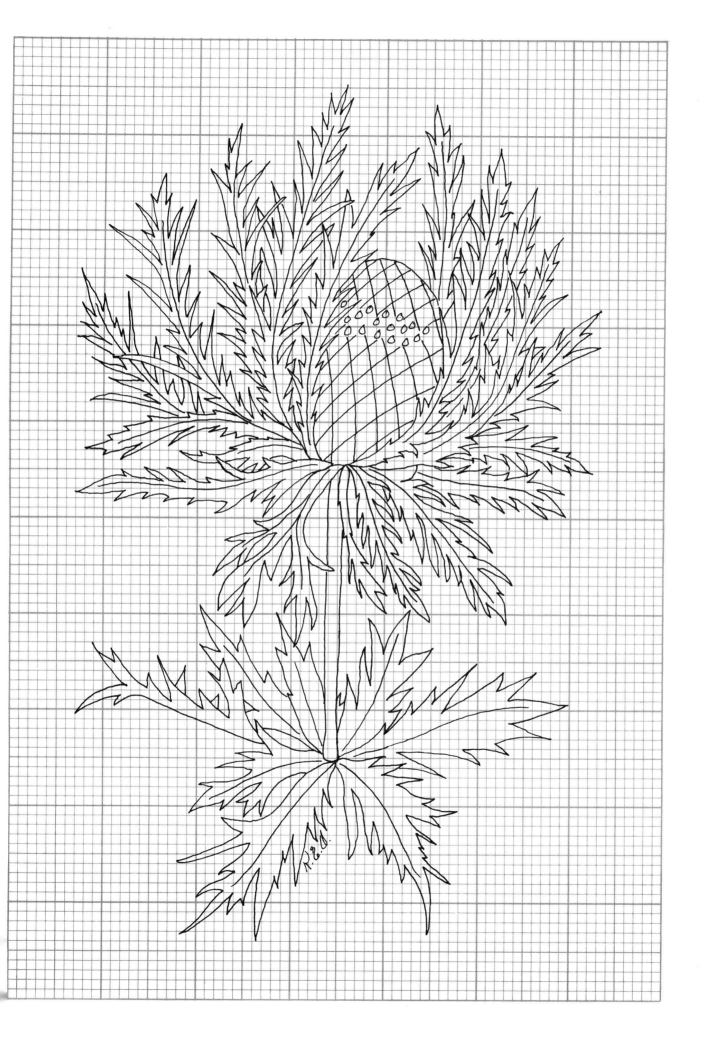

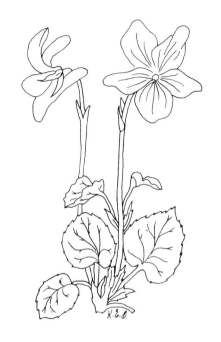

Pattern 43. Common Violet

The common wild violet, found throughout the United States and Europe, is a member of the pansy and violet family. (*Mountain Flowers*, Ill. 424, Text p. 288)

   The bloom is a blue-violet with white veining on the lower petal and a deep blue-violet veining on the other four petals. The "spur" at the back of the violet in profile is a pale blue tending toward white and sometimes yellow tones. The foliage is a rich green with touches of brown and the very base of the stems are roots in brown tones.

Pattern 44. Alpine Clematis

The heavy flower of the alpine clematis bends to earth much like the snowdrop. The coloring echos the common violets. The outer petals are lavender-blue with the inner petals surrounding the stamen white. The tips of the stamen are yellow and show only on the right flower. The stems of the flowers are brown and quite woody in texture. The leaves are a deep green with touches of olive and brown and the stem is distinctly green in contrast to the brown of the main branch and flower stems which surround it.

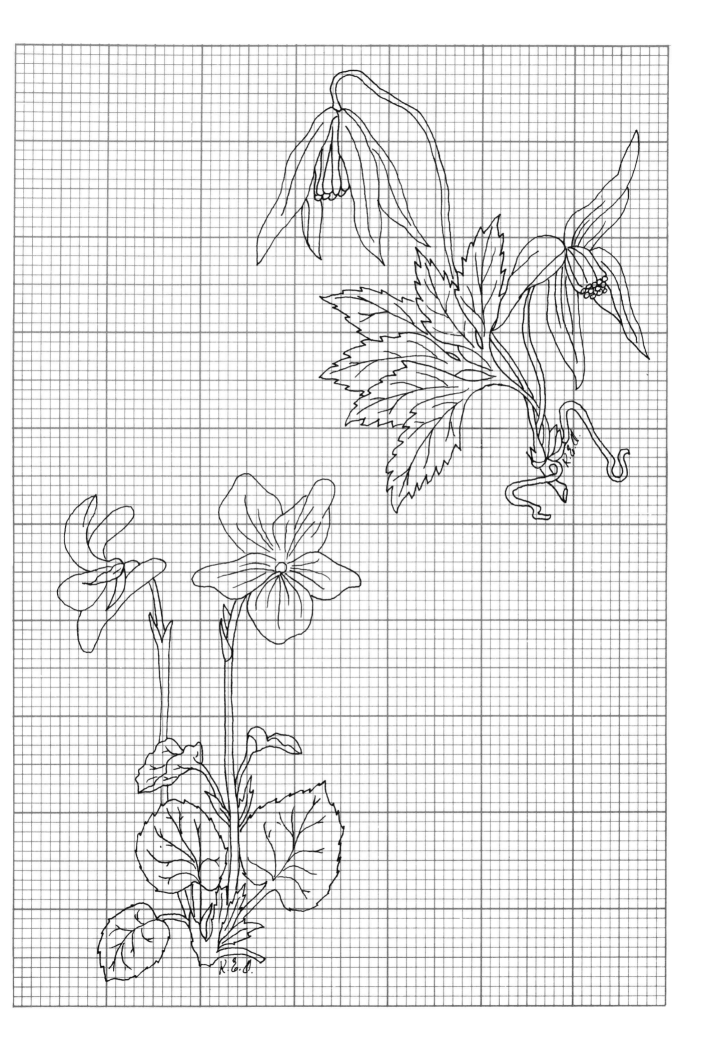

Pattern 45. Wild Strawberry #1

This pattern is a composite drawing of two varieties of wild strawberries. The fruit is taken from (*Mountain Flowers*, Ill. 292 and 293, Text p. 254). It is a member of the rose family.

The flowers of this delightful plant are white and widely parted with yellow centers and stamen and backed by green outer leaves which just show between the petals of the flower. The fruit, which is quite small when compared to the domestic strawberry, is a rich red with just a touch of yellow. The unripe fruit is a pale white-green developing into yellow-green and into the palest of peach colors before maturing when fully ripe to red. They are heavily seeded with brown seeds and often bend to the ground on brownish stems. The foliage is brown-green with touches of blue-green veining.

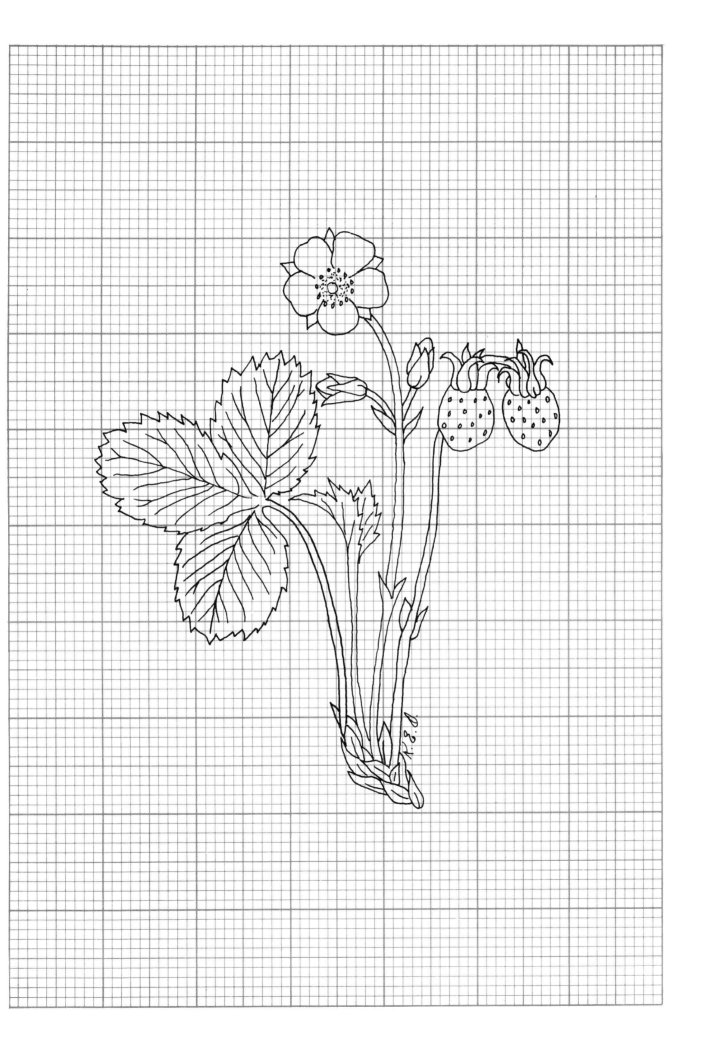

Pattern 46. Toothwort

The toothwort which is a member of the broomrape family and not to be confused with those "worts" which are a member of the Cress Family. (*Mountain Flowers,* Ill. 681, Text p. 352)

The plant grows in the woods on the roots of some trees much like the fungus. It's texture is fleshy and the coloring varies from white to a pale, pale pink. The flowers tend to have just the subtlest tint of violet to the slightly deeper pink petals.

The plant is rare and grows at higher elevations in Great Britain.

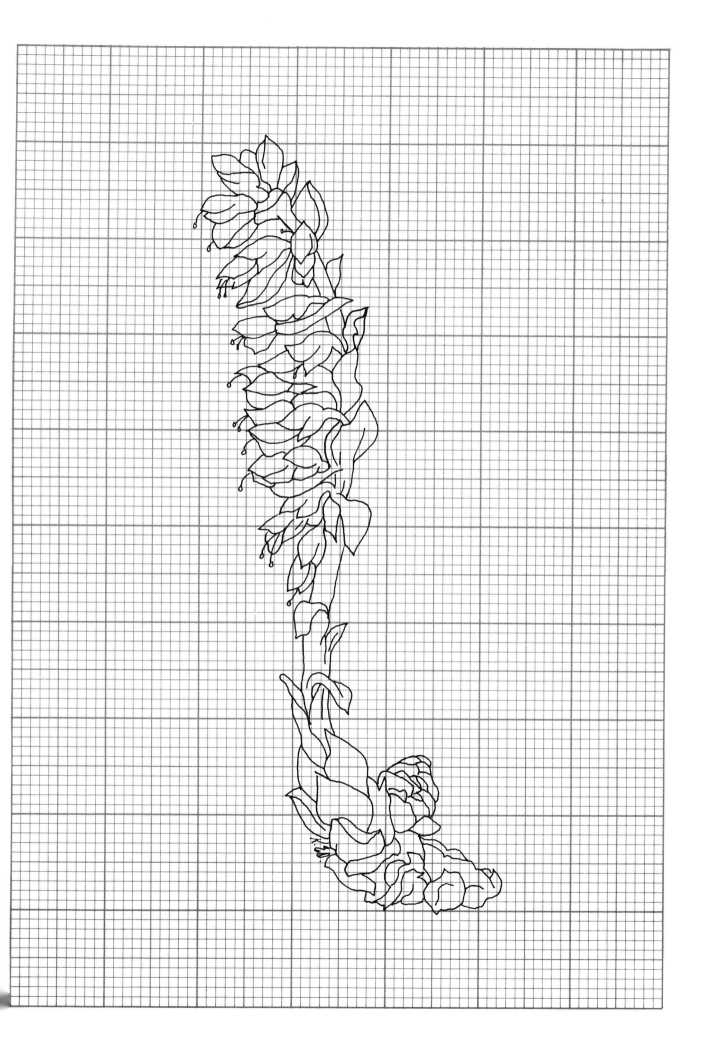

Pattern 47. Raspberry

Raspberries, a member of the rose family, are common to the wilds in the United States and Europe. (*Mountain Flowers,* Ill. 1047, Text p. 253)

Two varieties are common in the woods around New Hampshire—the red raspberry and the black raspberry. Both look similar to this illustration except that the berries are different colors.

The foliage on both varieties tends to bluish tones of green with very thorny and rather woody stems, both in texture and coloring. The leaves are rather hairy on both sides and distinctively veined.

The raspberry bloom is white with just the barest touches of pink on the petals and a yellow center. The green outer leaves frame the bloom.

The red raspberry fruit has a deep "raspberry" red coloring when fully ripe and looks quite red from a distance. It tends to be more delicate to the touch and will drop away from the bush at the slightest brush of your hand leaving behind the center core which is a pale yellow-brown in color. It tends to grow quite brown the longer the fruit has been gone.

The black raspberry is really a very dark purple which looks black from a distance. The ripening fruit varies from pale green to red to deep purple— all on the same berry. It ripens from the tip toward the stem.

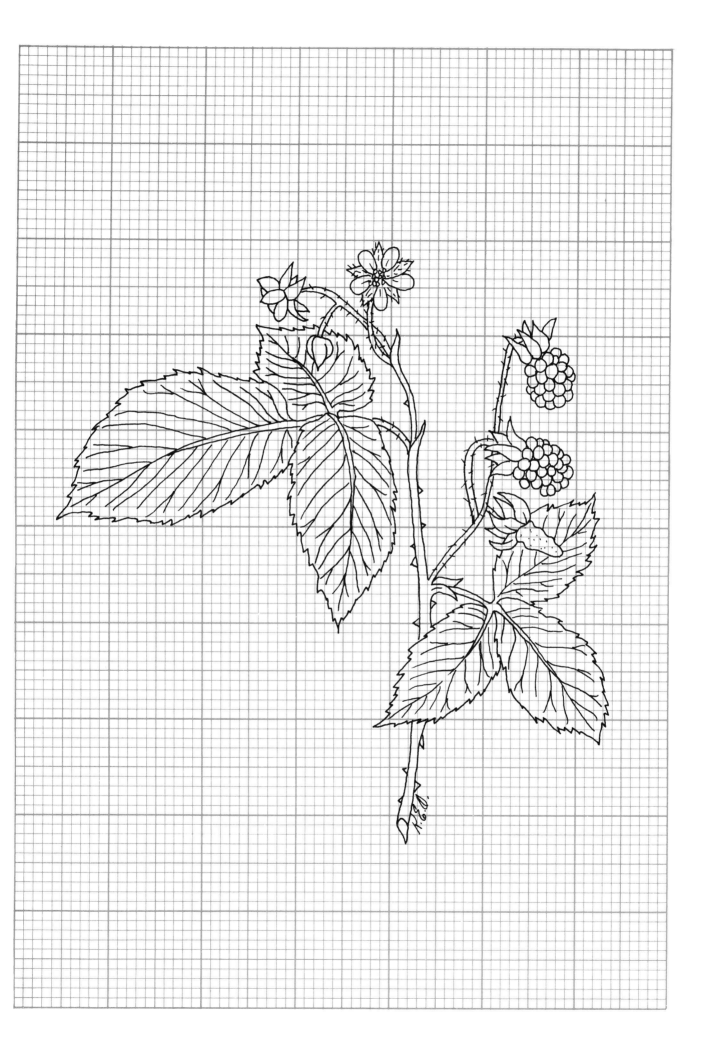

Pattern 48. Alpine Rose

The alpine rose is very similar to the cow pasture rose found in the New England area. (*Mountain Flowers*, Ill. 281, Text p. 251)

The thorns on the alpine rose are small and often nonexistent, leaving a smooth stem. The leaves are also smooth and rather bright green or yellow-green. The flower is a bright pink with a touch of purple. It has a yellow center and yellow stamen thickly packed at the center.

Because so many of the wild roses look similar, it is possible to change the coloring of the flower and have a rose of an entirely different name. Coloring possibilities among the wild varieties include: pale yellow petals, green center, and bright yellow stamen bordering on brown; the palest tints of pink ranging from the yellow tones through the slightly lavender, with yellow center and stamen; and white bloom with green center, yellow stamen, and many prickles on the stems.

Notice that this pattern can be used horizontally as well as vertically as it is illustrated.

Pattern 49. Edelweiss

The edelweiss, made immortal in the song in *The Sound of Music,* is a member of the daisy family. (*Mountain Flowers,* Ill. 779, Text p. 376)

The plant, including the petals of the blossom, is fuzzy all over. The blossom is white with a muted mustard-colored center. The leaves tend to be blue-green on brownish stalks. The overall coloring is very pale although the plant itself is quite sturdy and stiff, not at all delicate like its coloring.

Because the plant is so wooly in texture, you might consider doing turkey work on a good portion of it with other highly textured stitches as accents.

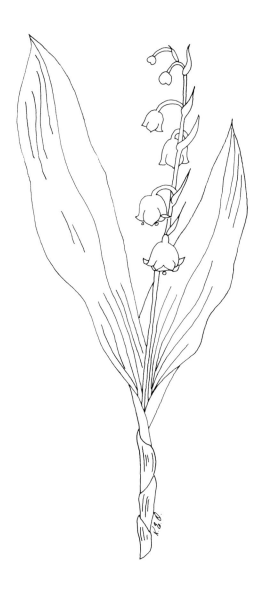

Pattern 50. Lily of the Valley #2

This lily of the valley pattern is a true relative of the lily family. (*Mountain Flowers,* Ill. 891, Text p. 170)

This botanical drawing is very different from the abstracted version in Pattern 12.

The lily of the valley is always white and ages to a cream color. The green foliage is very deep and rich. The stems are very stiff and a lighter tone of green than the leaves.

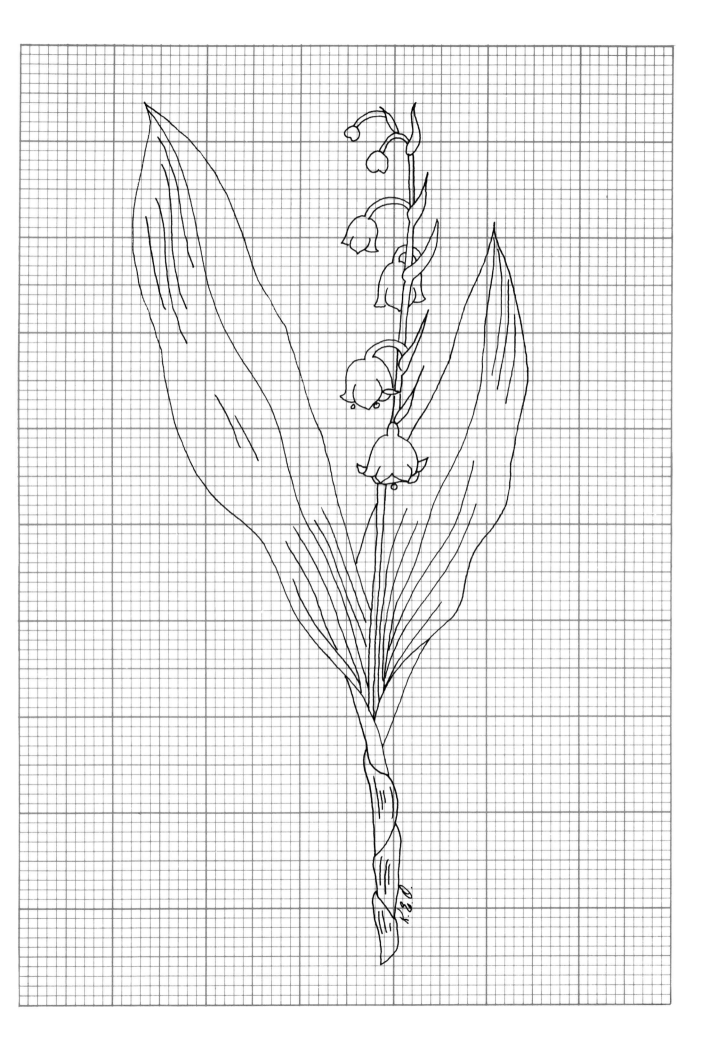

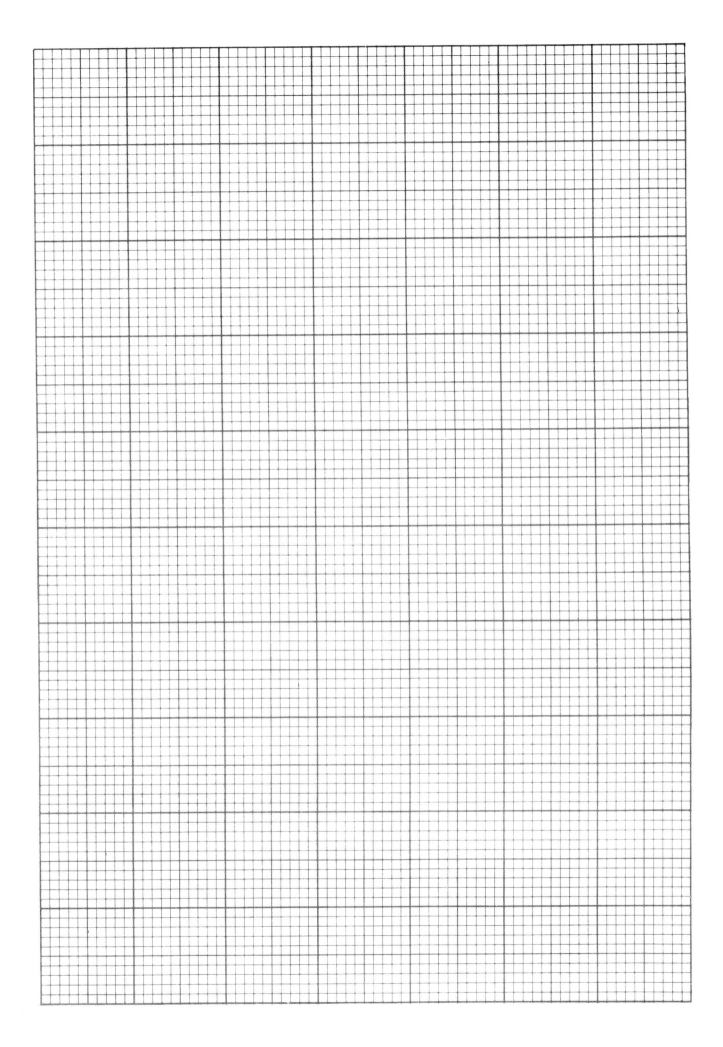

CHAPTER 7:

Mary Vaux Walcott Flowers

The National Collection of Fine Arts that is connected with the Smithsonian Institution in Washington, D.C., is a fine resource. It houses and maintains the fine-arts materials that have been given to our nation. Among this collection of priceless artwork are over eight-hundred paintings by Mary Vaux Walcott, a special collection of which was published in *North American Wildflowers*.

Patterns 51 through 65 are my line drawings abstracted from these paintings. I have occasionally flopped the illustration, consolidated the flowers, or eliminated details to show off the plant better. The originals, however, should be seen if you visit Washington, D.C. Just contact the National Collection of Fine Arts for details on how to do this.

One other valuable resource is *Wild Flowers of America*, published by Crown Publishers, Inc. It contains a good selection of Walcott paintings in color with additional paintings by Dorothy Falcon Platt. The illustrations are large and useful for needlework.

Pattern 51. Mountain Lady's Slipper

The mountain lady's slipper is a member of the orchid family and grows wild in the woods of the northwest United States and Canada.

The sepals, which fall just beind the pouch of the slipper, are twisted and dark green to a brownish purple. The slipper is white with pink or very slightly purple veining.

The leaves, textured by quite dark veining, tend to be gray tones of green.

Just at the top of the slipper is a yellow petal which appears like an upper short lip just above the pouting lower one which we identify as the slipper.

Pattern 52. Bloodroot

The bloodroot is a member of the poppy family and derives its name from the bright red sap found in the roots of the plant.

The petals of the flower are white with a bright yellow center tinged slightly with orange. A touch of green identifies a piston in the center. The foliage is a soft green which tends toward brown at the base; the leaves at the very base are brown.

Pattern 53. Yellow Lady's Slipper

The yellow lady's slipper is another member of the orchid family that abounds in the woods of the northern United States and southern Canada. The outer sepals are twisted and vary in coloring from greenish yellow to brownish purple and frame a slipper which is in the paler tones of mustard yellow. The leaves are dark green and heavily veined.

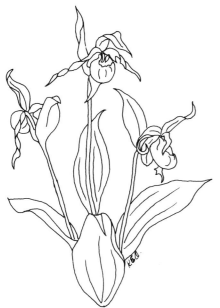

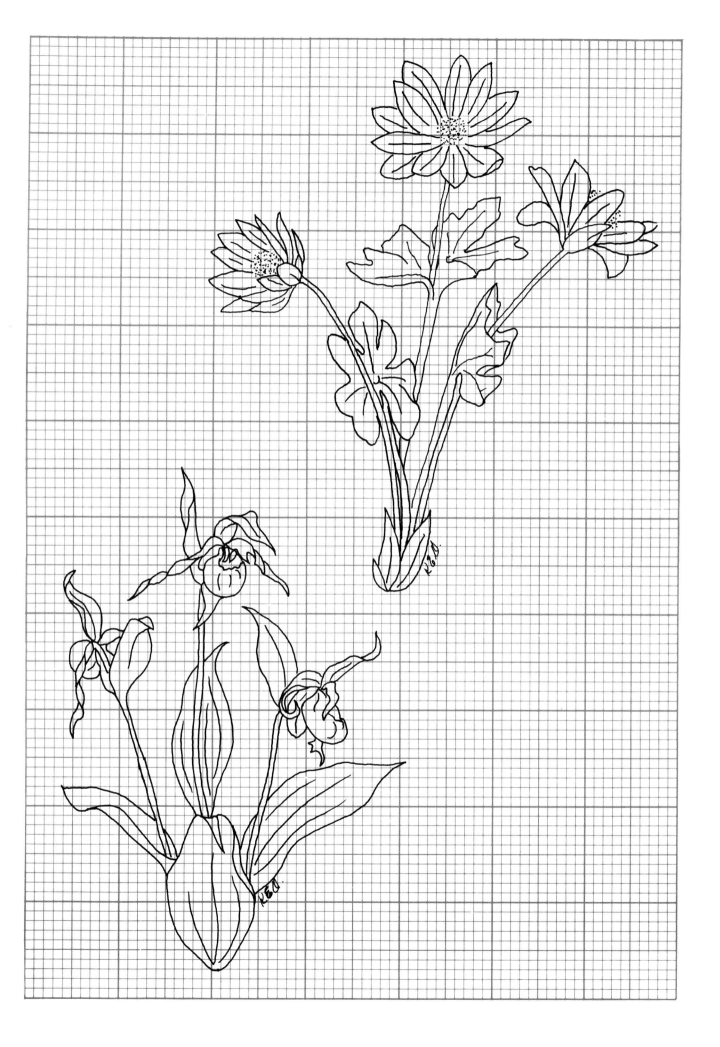

Pattern 54. Bellwort

The bellwort is a member of the mariposa lily family. The flowers are pale yellow-green and look very much like lilies. The soft green foliage has touches of yellow-green and distinct dark green veining. The stems, which seem to pierce the leaves, are quite yellow-green close to the flowers and turn brown down toward their bases.

Pattern 55. Bride's Bonnet

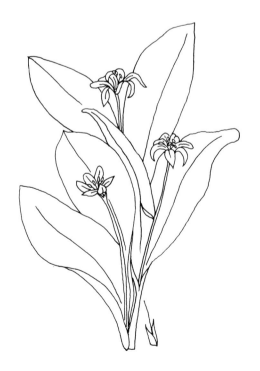

Bride's bonnet or queen's cup is another member of the mariposa lily family that is found in the high mountains of the Pacific Northwest north into Alaska. The flowers are white with slight grayish shading toward the center. The stamens are brown. The leaves are a deep lush green with a heavy yellowish green vein running up the center. The stems of the flowers and the leaves become brown as they reach the ground.

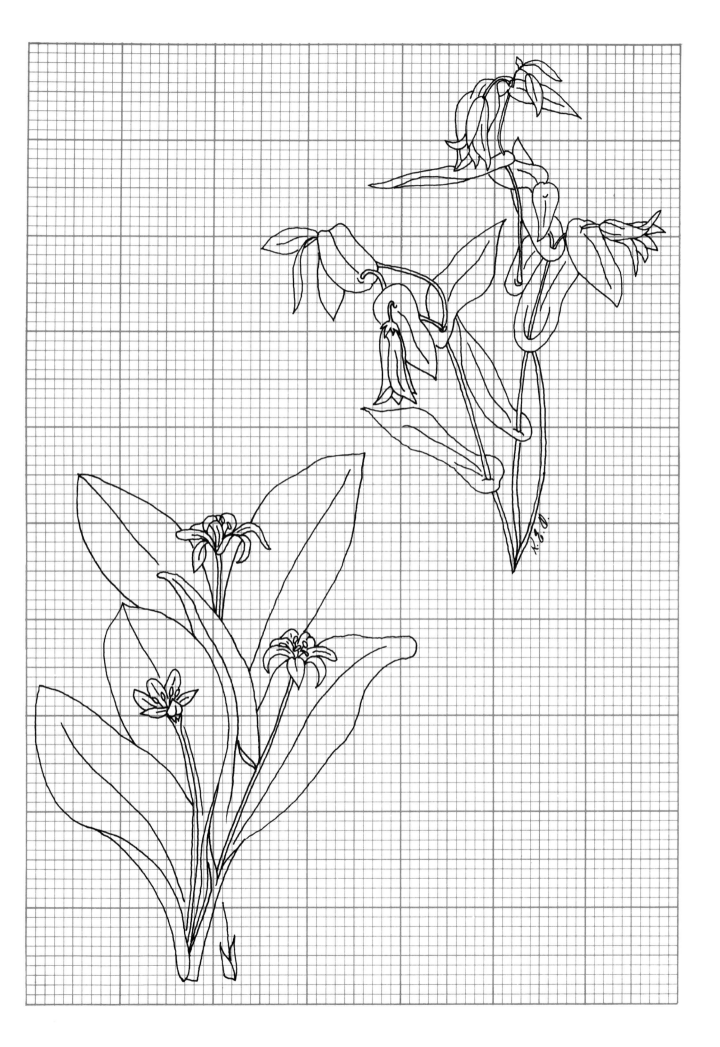

Pattern 56. Yellow Columbine

The yellow columbine is a member of the buttercup family and grows wild in the Western United States. Hybrids are grown in wildflower gardens around the world.

The flower is pure yellow ranging from the palest yellow to a rather bright buttercup. Some of the plants are touched with the slightest hint of red on the outer petals.

The foliage is a soft green with a grayish blue cast to the slightly fuzzy leaves. The veining is greenish white with a chalk white center area.

I have one of the very pale yellow versions in my garden. The stems are slim and weighed down by the blooms which dance at the slightest breath of air.

The stamens are quite green terminating in tiny yellow collections of pollen balls.

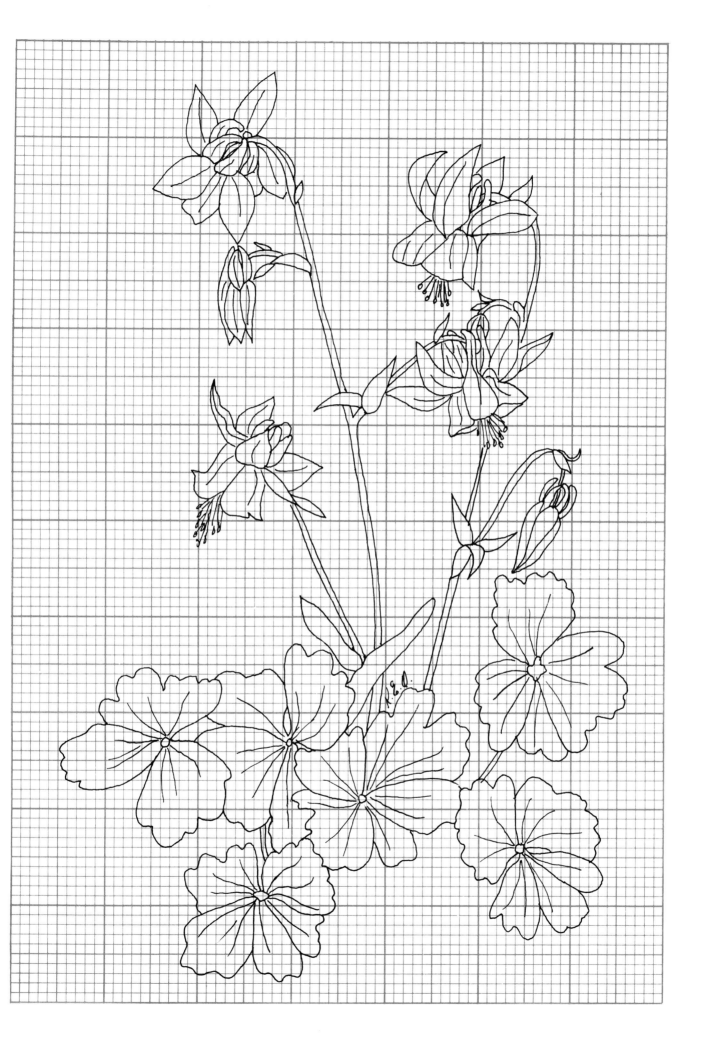

Pattern 57. Wild Rose

The many species of wild rose are so diverse that you can change the coloring slightly and have another variety of rose.

This red variety has a bright yellow stamen on richly green-yellow leaves. The stems are woody and brown and heavily thorned.

If you skip ahead to Chapter 10, you will see how to use this pattern to make a large, very full panel by flopping the illustration and fitting the angles together.

The natural colors of wild roses include yellows, whites, pinks, and reds. The centers vary from yellows to greens; the stamens are usually bright yellow, The leaves can have an olive or blue-green cast depending on the variety. Although the leaf forms and size vary slightly, I think any botanist will give you poetic license.

Pattern 58. Red Columbine

The wild columbine, which grows around the New Hampshire woods, has red outside petals and a yellow underskirt called sepals. It is a member of the buttercup family.

The foliage is somewhat different from the full-shaped leaves of the yellow columbine. They are gray green, separated distinctly, and less compact. The darker green veining ends at the juncture with the stems.

The stems of this variety are thinner and browner in color than the other varieties giving the heavy blooms little support from the breezes.

Other varieties of columbine have blue or violet outside petals and yellow sepals; pink outside petals and yellow under sepals; and combinations of outside petals including white and pastel colors of red, pink, yellow, blue, and lavender.

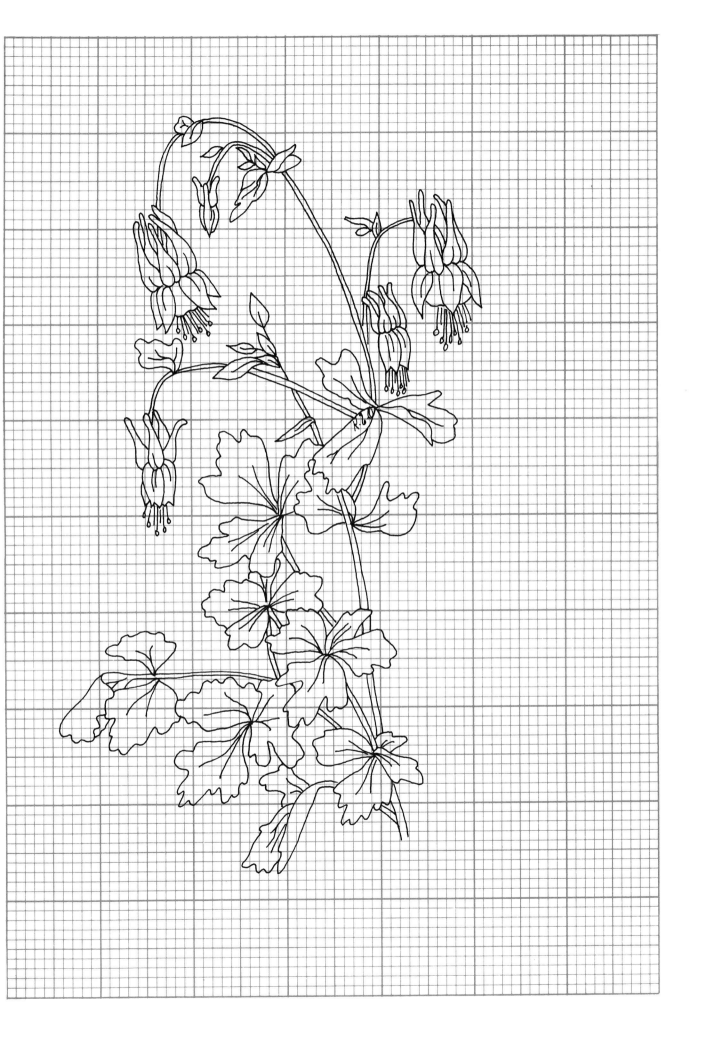

Pattern 59. Pinks #1

The combination of patterns on this page is just an example of how you can work two different patterns together.

The Wild Pink in the upper portion of the drawing does not have to be pink. It varies from white to a very dark pink bordering on a red, is a member of the pink family, and grows abundantly in the New Hampshire area. In the Walcott paintings the palest gray-pink petals come together to a grayish and white center. The throats of the flowers are slightly greenish and the "collar" of the stem is quite brown at the juncture of the flower and a deep brown on the entire stem. The leaves have a yellow-green tone and a dark vein up the center.

Pattern 60. Painted Trillium

The painted trillium in the bottom portion of the drawing is the most dramatic in coloring of the trillium family. The white flower has a series of red or purple veins coming from a quite yellow and green center. The foliage is rather an olive green with a contrasting pale green veining brown-green stems. Other varieties of trillium have single colored flowers in white or purple either brilliant yellow or yellow and purple centers contrasting with white outer petals.

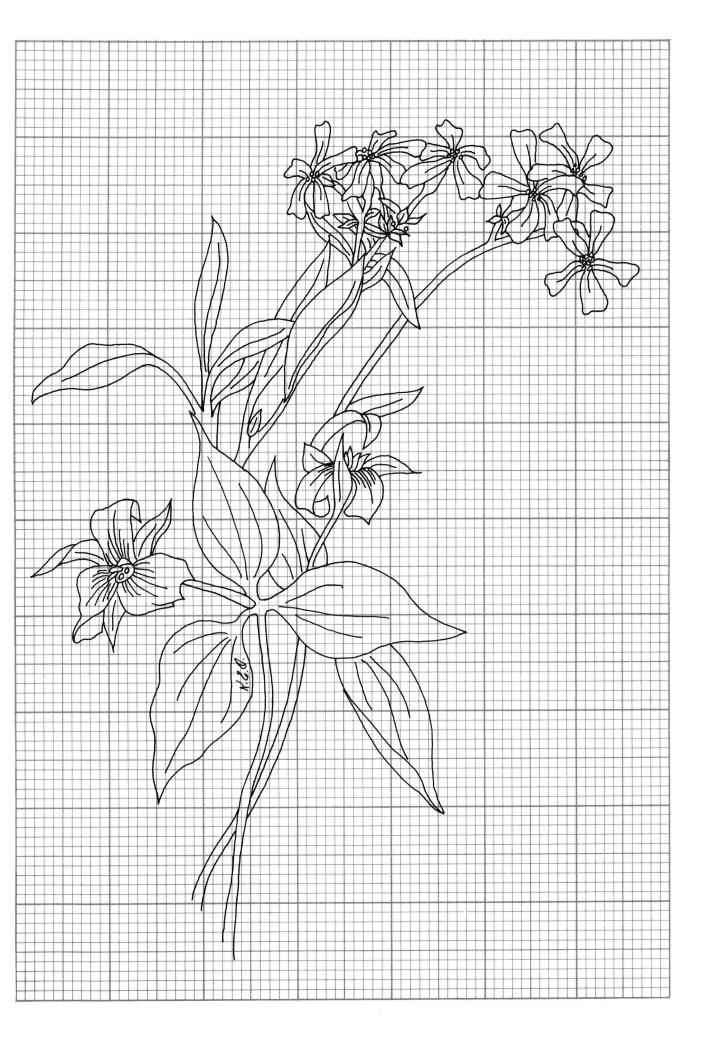

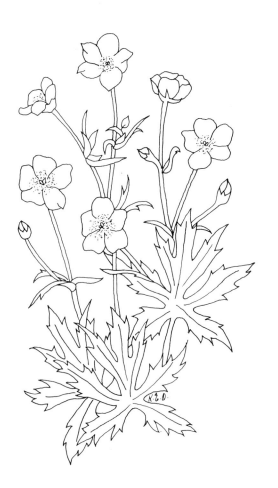

Pattern 61. Tall Buttercups

The tall buttercup dots the fields throughout the United States with gay yellow blooms. The rather shiny petals may have tempted you, as they did me, as a child to hold the blossom under the chins of friends to see if they liked butter. The reflection of yellow off the shiny leaves of the petals usually indicated that they did, indeed.

Some varieties have rather white petals, but most are very yellow and have become associated with that color for generations. The foliage is quite dark in comparison and tends to be rather bluish in the Walcott paintings.

I have indicated the stamens with tiny dots, however, the original painting indicates a center of very short and stiff stamens that appear to look like miniature dandelions at the center of the flower. This may give you an idea for selecting a more textured center stitch than the seeding of my drawing.

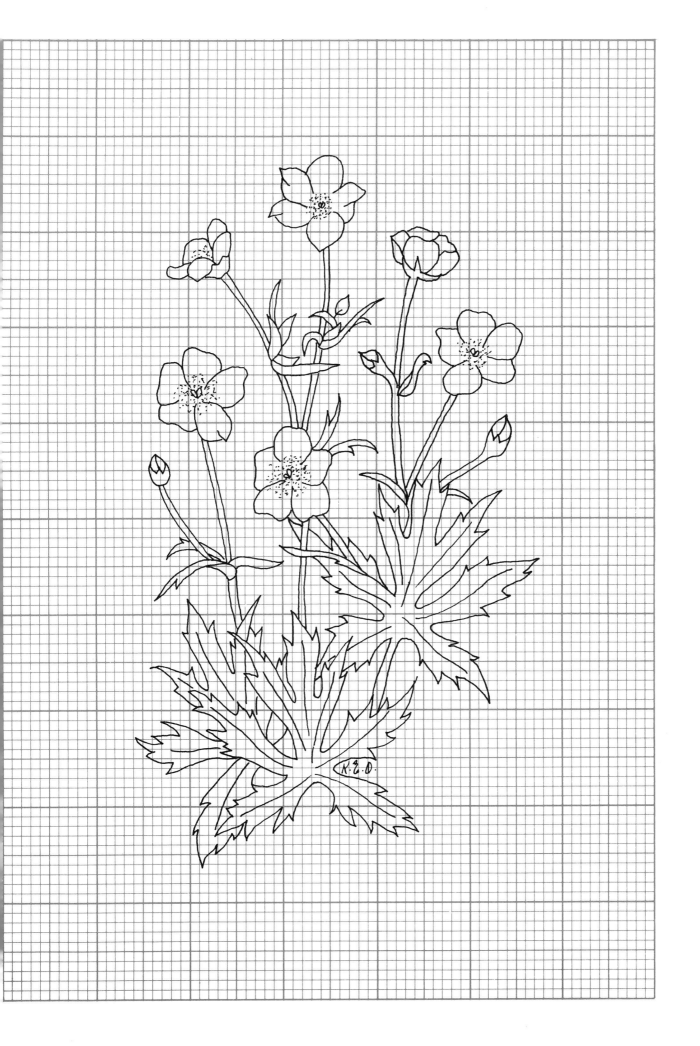

Pattern 62. Rhododendron

The rhododendron comes in many variations and, of course, belongs to the rhododendron family which also includes the azalea. The basic difference is that the rhododendron is evergreen but the azalea drops its leaves in winter.

Rhododendron come in many colors including white with just a touch of pink at the tips of each petal and matching stamen, a bright purplish pink petal with white and yellow stamen; and variations of pink and lavender flowers. The foliage is stiff, smooth to the touch, and a deep rich hunter green with very dark veining.

The bush or shrub is quite woody and tends to be brownish green with very distinct joints where the old leaves have dropped off.

Pattern 63. Iris #2

The large blue flag iris is quite different from the shorter variety in Pattern 38 of the same iris family.

For coloring details see Pattern 38. The Walcott painting is done in lavender tones with touches of yellow—almost ocre—at the center of the bottom petals and very dark, bordering on black purple, veining. The top petals are very light with hints of pinkish lavender in the shade of the creases.

The foliage is quite green with soft brown leaves at the joints of the flower stems.

To change this pattern to a yellow iris, first eliminate the veining, and add a touch of brown along the center veins and extending only in short lines around these center veins. The rest of the bloom is yellow with perhaps a touch of brown in the shadows for accent.

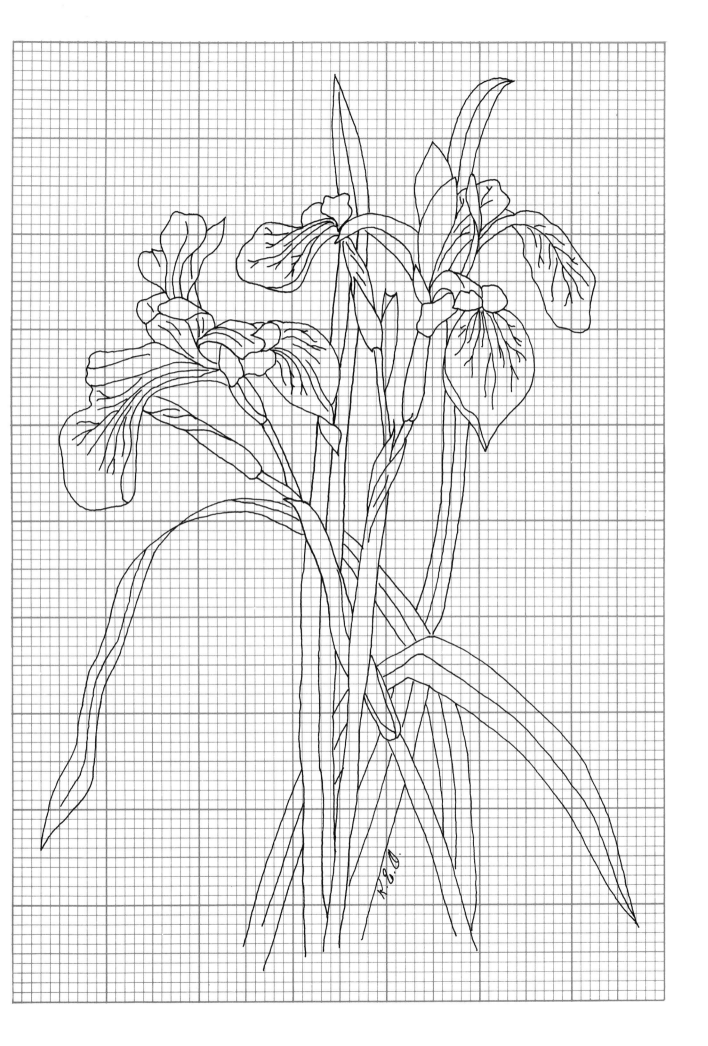

Pattern 64. Avalanche Lily

The avalanche lily is a member of the dog-tooth violet sub-family of the lily family. It is found only in the Pacific Northwest of the United States.

The coloring of this flower is delicate and white with just a touch of light mauve-pink along the outer center veins of the outside petals. The center of the inside petals is a deep mustard yellow which extends perhaps one quarter the length of the petal. The veining is lengthwise and pronounced with soft silvery gray shadowing. The back of the flower in the upper right part of the drawing echos the yellows toward the stem that are shown on the inside of the bloom. The stamens are a sharp mustard. yellow.

The stalk of the flower terminates at the bloom in slightly brownish pink tones and fades into a very prominent yellow-green with the final bud in a soft white-green with touches of yellow-green accents.

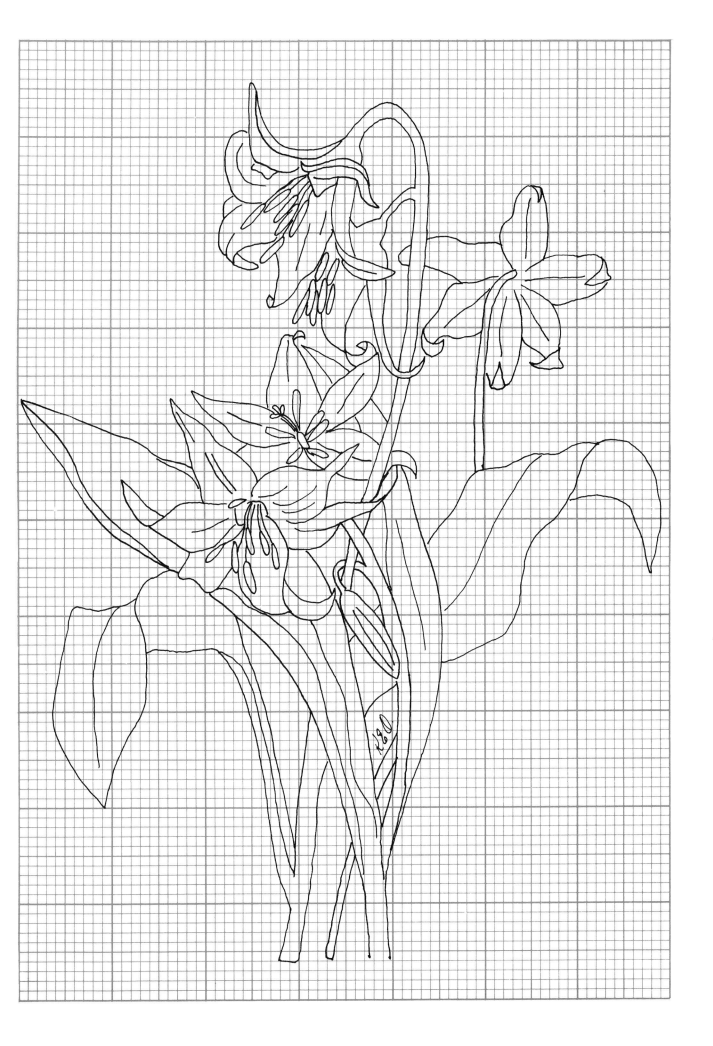

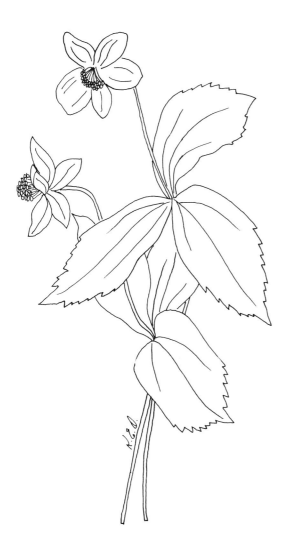

Pattern 65. Columbia Windflower

The columbia windflower, an anemone, is a member of the buttercup family.

This flower is white with yellow seeds and green stems. The long stem which reaches into a cluster of three leaves is slightly brown just before the leaves and quite brown as it passes the cluster of leaves to the ground.

The foliage is brownish green but not dark in coloring. The veins are a deeper shade of the same color and include some branching not shown in this illustration.

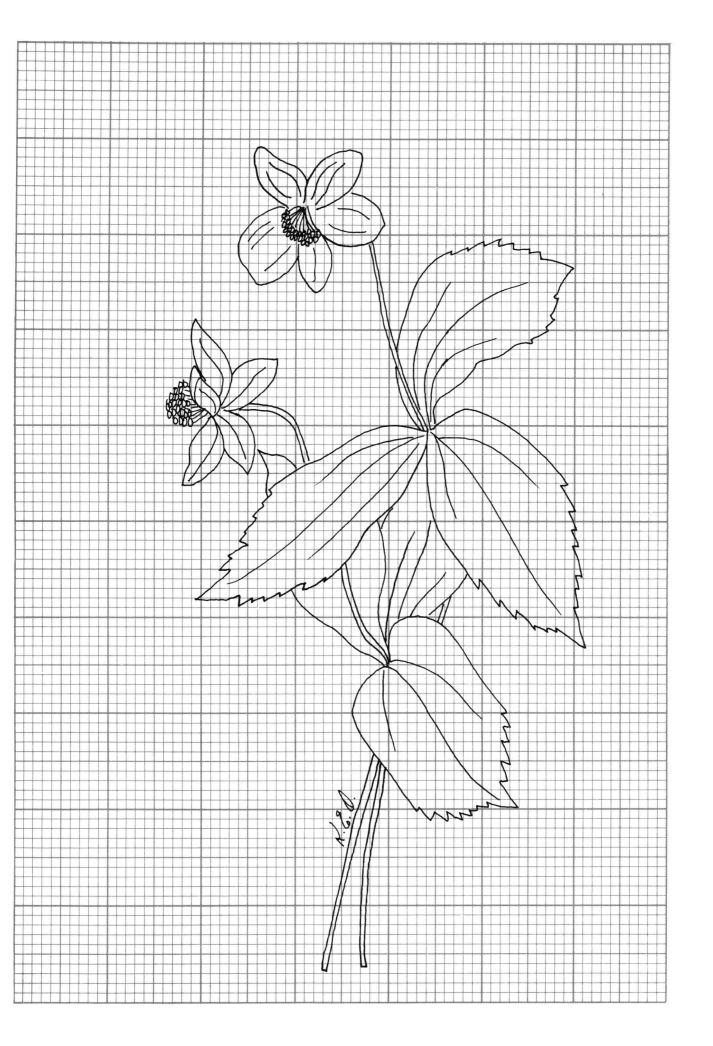

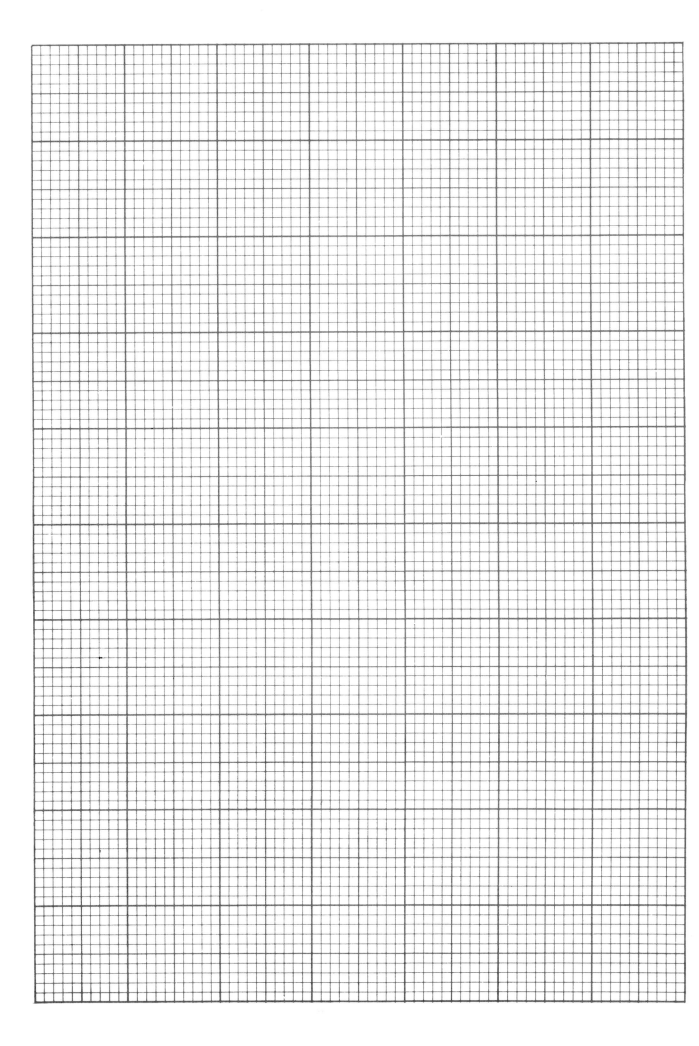

CHAPTER 8:

Millefleur Tapestries

This chapter will probably surprise you when you discover that the millefleur tapestries from which this entire collection of patterns has been selected were woven between A.D. 1400—1600. Millefleur simply means thousands of flowers which refers to the backgrounds of these famous tapestries.

Among the most famous of the millefleur tapestries are The Unicorn Tapestries which are housed by the Metropolitan Museum of Fine Arts at the Cloisters in New York City. The best resource book for the display of colors and style of the millefleur is *The Unicorn Tapestries* by Margaret B. Freeman, published by the Metropolitan Museum of Fine Arts. The photographs are large and the color reproduction, superb

As you will learn from Margaret Freeman's book, all the flowers are symbolically used in these tapestries. I have, however, taken as good a guess as possible at the modern flower and given you the coloring for the contemporary name so that you can utilize your botanical books for current coloring ideas. There are definitely times when I wish I had studied botany. This series of florals has produced one illustration for which I am "stumped." When you spot it, let me know if you know what it is called. I have simply taken a guess at two of the possible families it might be related to by virtue of the shape of the flower and leaves.

Pattern 66. Wild Strawberry #2

This is the second wild strawberry pattern. For detailed information refer back to Pattern 45.

Strawberries are a very popular theme throughout the millefleur tapestries and the coloring is almost always of the fully ripe berries.

Pattern 67. Yellow Pimpernel

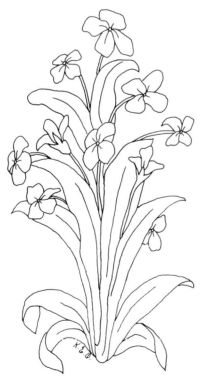

The yellow pimpernel, a member of the primrose family, is famous in literature in its "male" form, the scarlet pimpernel. In The Unicorn Tapestries the red variety predominates; however, I did find this one plant with yellow petals, red centers, and deep green foliage.

The scarlet pimpernels are very red with yellow centers. To emulate the coloring of the old tapestries, you could use a deep rich blue-green background and silhouette the flowers.

Pattern 68. Hawthorn

The flowers of the wild hawthorn shrub are white with red centers against a deep toned and rich foliage in blue-green. They fade quickly into almost a golden white at the tips of the leaves. There is much lore about the hawthorn and Margaret Freeman discusses it in *The Unicorn Tapestries*.

Pattern 69. Pinks #2

This is the second pattern of pinks. Those in the millefleur tapestries tend to be only pink and red with the center colors varying from yellow to red to greenish browns. Pattern 75 is another version of pinks.

Pattern 70. White Violet

The white violet in the United States is found as the sweet white violet. It is white with reddish stems; the very center seeding of the flower is purple. If you wish to interpret this flower as the northern white violet, make the seeds green.

Pattern 71. Jack-o-Lantern

Pattern 71 is known universally as the Chinese lantern, but I grew up knowing it as the Jack-o-lantern which we gathered in the late fall and brought in to dry over the winter. They are deep orange with an olive tint to the foliage and, indeed, look like Chinese lanterns used at a garden party.

Pattern 72. Yellow Violets

The yellow violet is identified in the United States as the "stemless" yellow violet. The petals are yellow with a hint of brown veining on the lower center petal. The foliage tends to hug the ground and "stemless" refers to the fact that the flower is not on the same stem as the leaves. It is the only yellow violet in this category in the U.S.

Pattern 73. Unknown

This is the mystery plant referred to earlier. In the tapestries it is an orange flower with brown center; the outside of the flower below the open petals is green as are the foliage and stems. By its shape it could be a member of either the gentian family or the bellflower group, which are blue, but I have found no reference to this particular coloring in either.

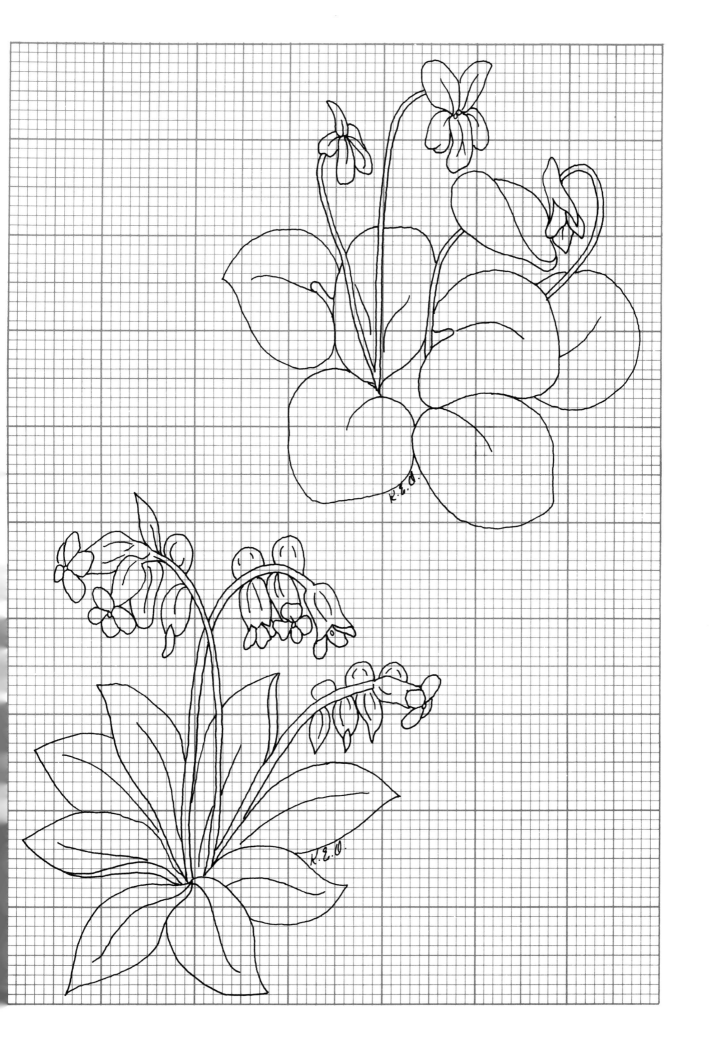

Pattern 74. Clary

I identified this flower as the clary from Margaret Freeman's book. The species belongs to the *Salvia* family and was popular and exotic in the tapestries. The coloring is particularly subtle.

The flowers, which remind me of the turtlehead, are very pale pink, almost white, with touches of slightly deeper pink along the outside edges of the blossom. The foliage is a very deep green with blue tones and almost a yellow-white highlighting. The pods are the same deep green with shading and again highlighted in very light tones.

The red turtlehead wildflower is the closest American plant to follow for floral detail. However, the coloring of our wildflower is very deep reddish pink. The turtlehead is a member of the snapdragon family.

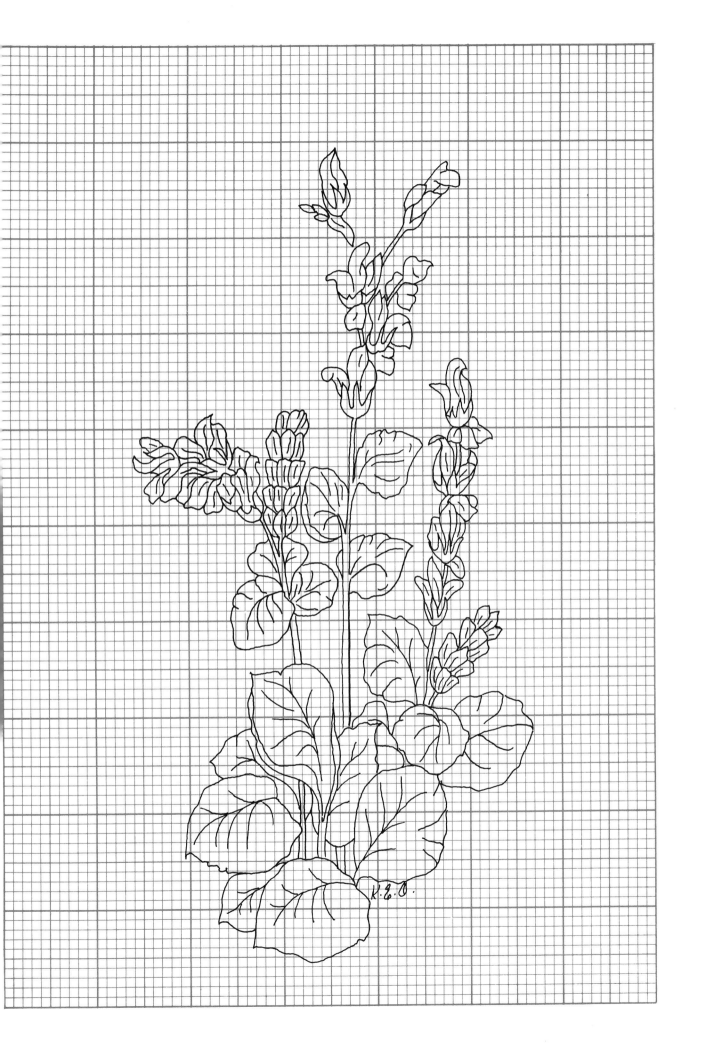

Pattern 75. Pinks #3

This is a taller version of pinks than shown in Pattern 69. The two patterns blend well and can be used in the same project.

In Medieval times, when these tapestries were made, pinks and carnations were based on the wild dianthus and illustrated in a similar manner. The carnations were usually red or white and represented engagement and marriage. The pinks were pink or red.

This pattern can easily be broken into three sections and rearranged into a pattern of your own design. See how two of the clumps extend from the base and the third is suspended above the base of leaves. These can be drawn separately and used as accents on another work.

In The Unicorn Tapestries these were red with white centers and with a tiny dot of yellow at the very center. The foliage was very deep green.

Pattern 76. Common Sow-Thistle

This could be the common sow-thistle or prickly lettuce, whichever suits your taste. The foliage is similar and the bloom is somewhat compatible to both plants.

The original plant in the tapestries was white with a slight yellowish bloom with a green neck. The deep green foliage had a slight tint of olive green. Again, all highlights were dramatic with almost a pale yellow-tan for the lightest shade.

Thistles had a religious significance in Medieval times and so are quite common to all tapestries woven during this period.

I see no reason to restrict your coloring to that found in The Unicorn Tapestries. Thistles are beautifully colored in red-purples and deep rich greens; blue and purples with touches of brown; and yellow with a lovely yellow-green overcast to the foliage.

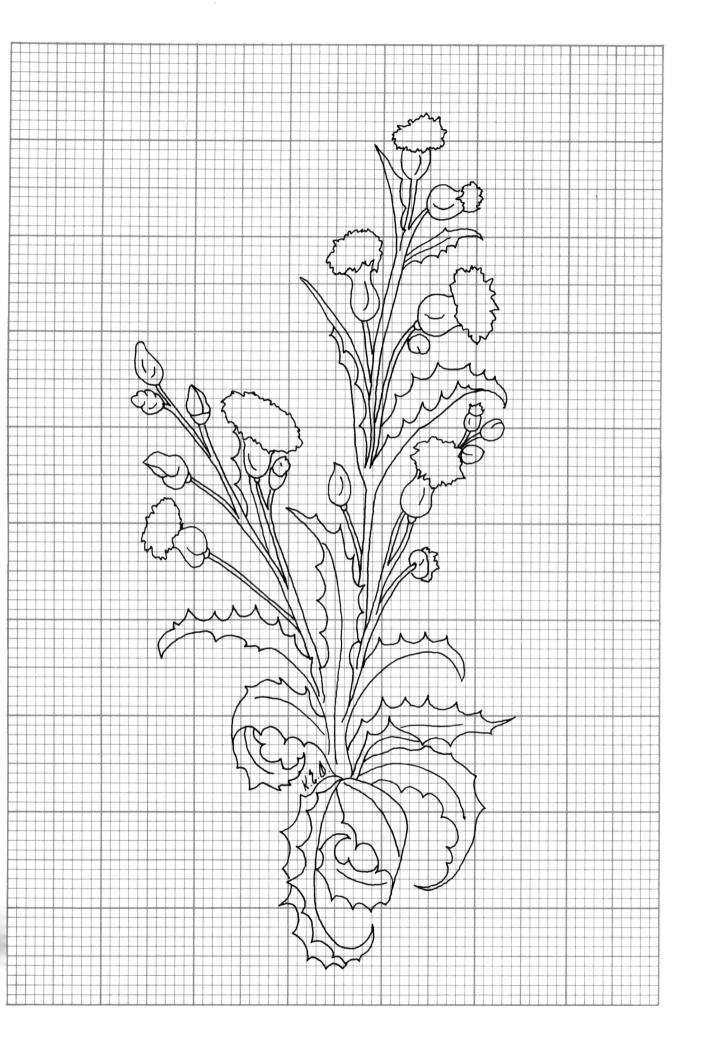

Pattern 77. Garden Phlox

The garden phlox is prolifically used in all colors throughout the Millefleur tapestries.

This particular group has white flowers with red centers and deeply rich green leaves and stems.

Garden phlox in the United States come in tones of pink with dark green centers and lavender with brownish green centers. The leaves have very pronounced center veins in a color lighter than the leaves and have evenly spaced side veining which goes almost to the tip of the leaf.

You can divide this pattern into two different ones by separating the foliage at the base.

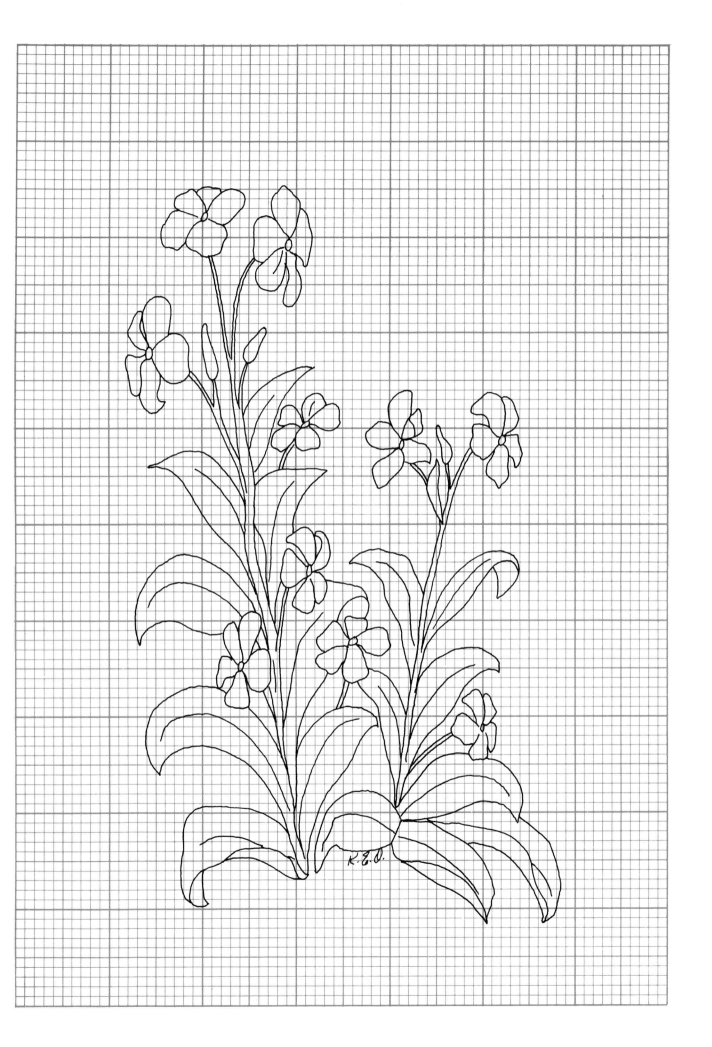

Pattern 78. Jonny Jump-ups

Jonny jump-ups, a relative of the violet family, have very distinct coloring not found in the other violet groupings.

The top two petals are a deep red-lavender and the bottom three are quite white with a tiny yellow center. The leaves are quite jagged and curled. The coloring again is deep yellow-green with highlighting almost to a cream color.

Should you prefer to make this pattern in traditional violet colors, see Patterns 2, 8, 43, 70, and 72 for coloring suggestions.

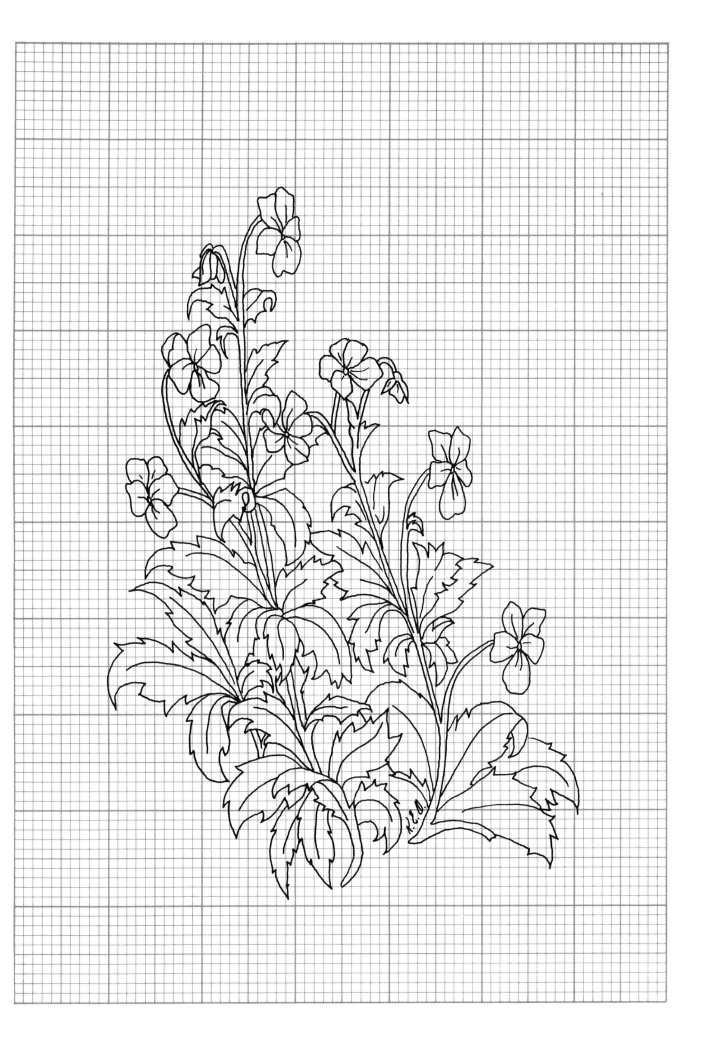

Pattern 79. Blue Periwinkle

The blue periwinkle, also called Vinca Minor, likes shade and spreads rapidly as a ground cover.

This plant was considered an herb in the Middle Ages and was thought to have a special power that could drive the Devil away.

The flowers are a lavender-blue for which the special color periwinkle blue is named. The foliage is yellowish green and possibly variegated with white, yellow, and yellow-green.

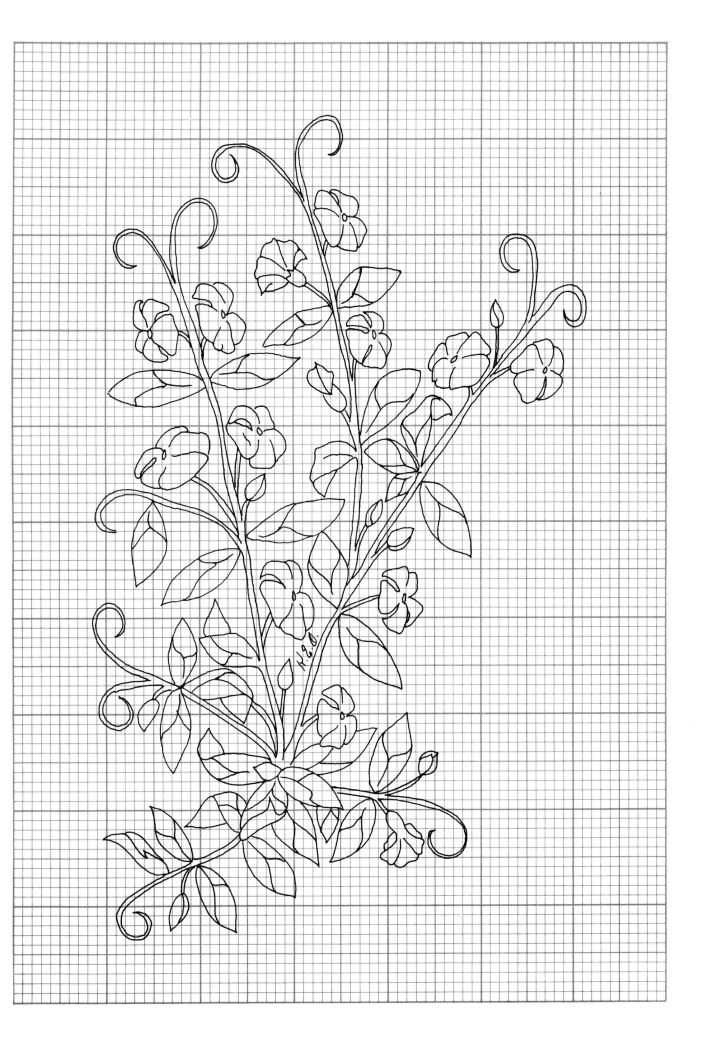

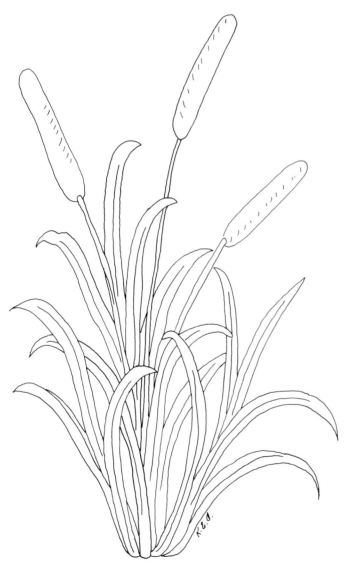

Pattern 80. Cattail Reeds

Cattail reeds were associated in the Medieval period with the Mocking of Christ in the *Bible*.

The heads of these reeds are brown and highly
textured as they comprise thousands of tiny flowers
tightly packed together. The feel is soft. Above
these sausage shapes are usually another thinner
and lighter in color set of flowers that are tightly
packed. As they fall off, a long needle-shaped spear
is left at the tip of the head. These spears are not
shown in the tapestry from which this drawing was
taken. The leaves are very stiff and tall and a deep
green.

This pattern is a good one to play with texture
stitches. You could do the entire flower in tiny
French knots and then use, perhaps, a cretan stitch
for some of the leaves, herringbone for others.

The stalks of the reeds remain a light tan-green
and are very smooth.

The plants are found in marshy areas.

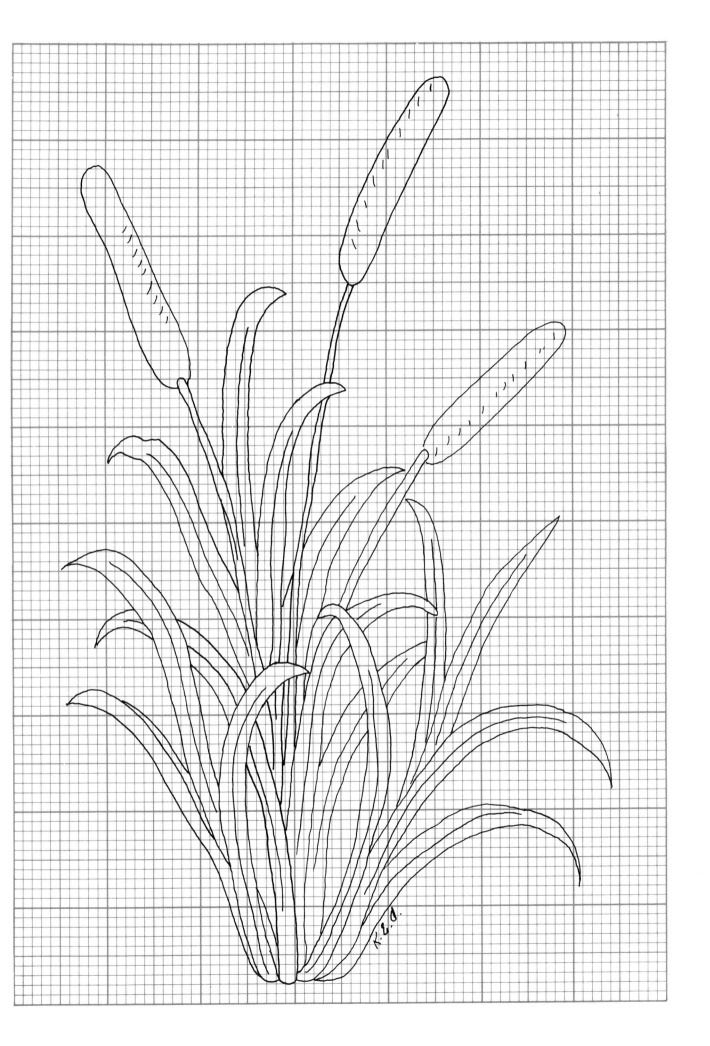

Pattern 81. Carnations #2

These carnations are more like wild pinks than are the carnations in Pattern 21. More information on pinks and carnations as they appear in the tapestries is given with Pattern 75.

The carnations here are pink and red with light yellow stamens. The foliage is rich in greens with very pale cream highlights.

You can separate different clusters of the design to use as details in other designs. Just notice where the flowers join the foliage and use that for your separation.

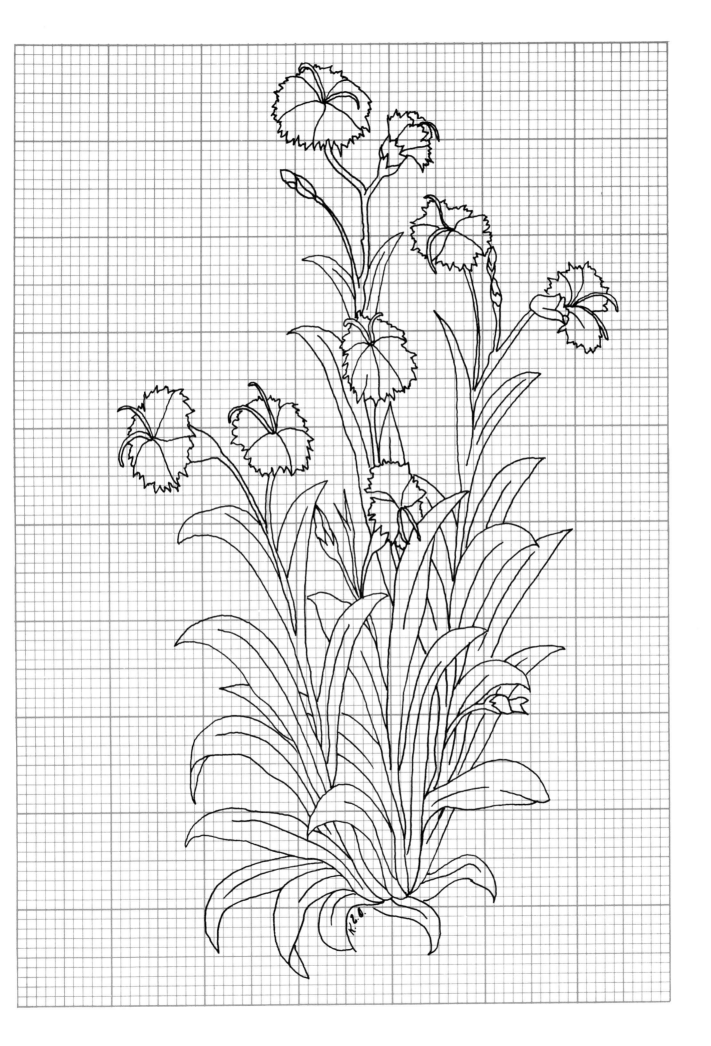

Pattern 82. Field Daisy or Marguerite

The field daisy is also known as the marguerite. The coloring is traditional with the white petals spotted here and there with touches of yellow. They have orange and brown centers and pale, soft green foliage. The buds are quite green and tipped with yellow where the flowers are just bursting through.

The shading is very dark in the tapestries with almost a hunter green color to the center veins which alternately turns cream color where it is in dark shadow.

Some of the other flowers which might be fun are: feverfew which has a large center "button" and somewhat stubbier petals but the coloring is similar; ox-eye daisy which has a white petal and yellow center that is depressed in the center; and for yellow flowers, the variations of the sunflowers, coneflower, and susan family are fun. You might refer back to Pattern 31 for more ideas.

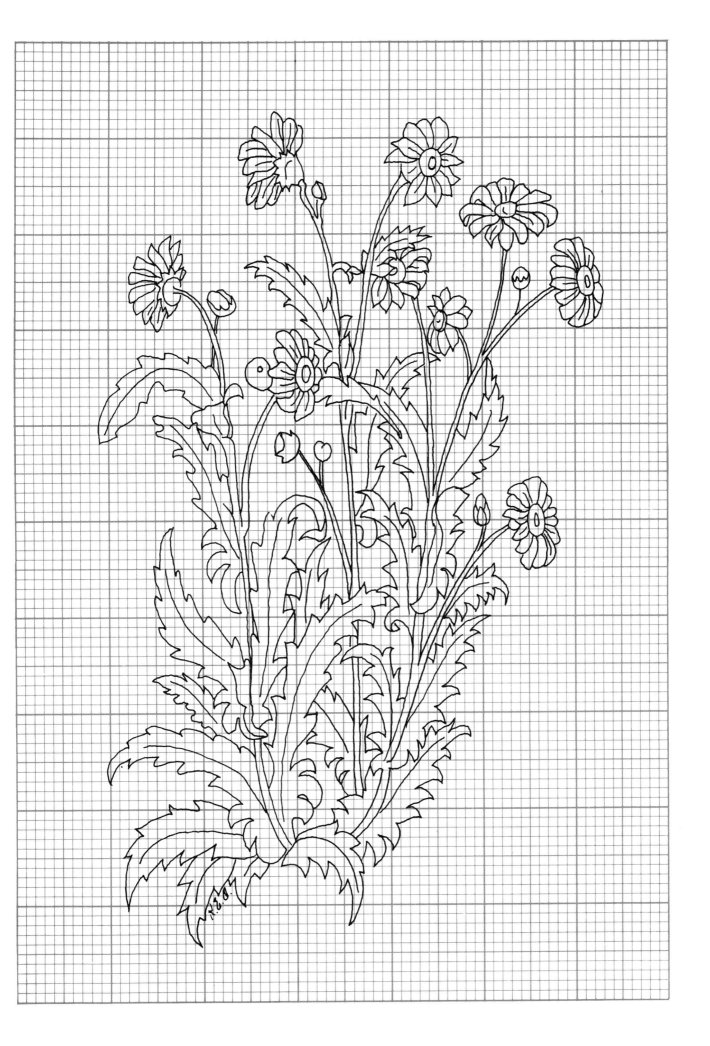

Pattern 83. Iris #3

This is the traditional iris which is found throughout the centuries as one of the most popular themes in the decorative arts. Other iris patterns are 38 and 63.

The Iris is the basis of the French fleur de lis, the symbol of royalty.

The coloring of this particular pattern was that of the blue flag iris described in Pattern 63.

Again you can separate this pattern into two different ones. Notice how the bottom cluster arches to the right and the cluster in the background arches to the left. Both are good compositions to use alone.

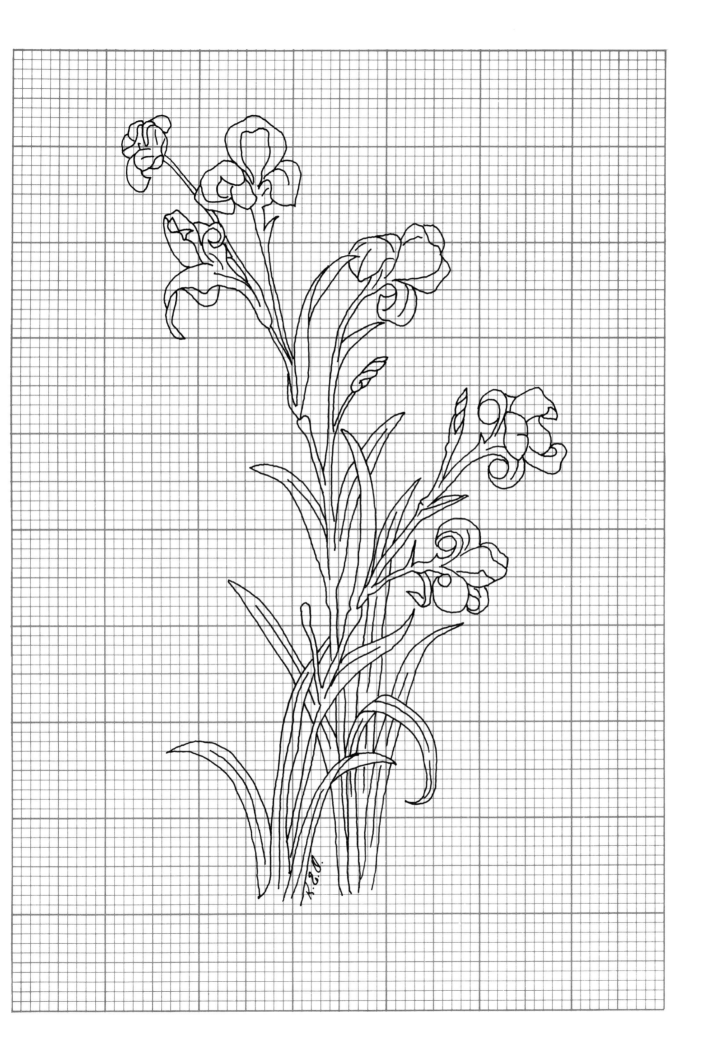

CHAPTER 9:

Jacobean Florals

The era of James I of England and the style of design that was popular during his reign is known as Jacobean. Jacobean designs were popular for almost one hundred years and formed the basis of the crewel embroidery patterns that were brought to the Colonies from England by early settlers. The style is primarily English and quite different from the French mille fleur works.

There appears to have been no rules for stitch or color selection, and the end results exploded with vitality. It is perhaps this freedom of expression that has helped to keep the essence of this period alive throughout the centuries.

Certain materials, however, did influence the tradition. The work was done on natural or bleached linens, usually of a twill weave. This fabric is strong and durable and was especially suitable for the home furnishings—upholstery, bedspreads, curtains, and other large, long-lifed projects—that were needlecrafted during this period.

Color preferences during the Jacobean period changed with the vogue of the day. However, green with many shadings and variations predominated. Important secondary themes within a composition were primarily in blues and browns. As the designs developed, they grew softer in tone with rose reds used little and black and gray, even less. The colors chosen were shaded in five to eight different values. Rather than being utilized in a

realistic manner, colors were randomly mixed demonstrating a pleasure in color rather than a painter's exacting eye. Greens, which flowed throughout the work, held the other fanciful color interpretations together.

In coloring the patterns you should suit your own sense of color and individual personality. If you wish to be completely contemporary in your color and stitch selection, your work will represent more closely the traditions of the Elizabethan period, which was the precursor of the Jacobean period. If you tend to a more antique look and controlled palette of stitches, your work will look more Jacobean or Colonial. The more inventive you become, the more the work will satisfy your own desire to express yourself.

The following patterns are chosen only from the traditional floral patterns of this period; the subject of Jacobean designs would fill an entire book of its own. They are all abstractions of actual flowers; some are classics of the period, others are more contemporary. Each flower name is given and may give you some ideas for coloring.

If this style of pattern pleases your taste, I suggest that you get Mildred Davis's *The Art of Crewel Embroidery,* published by Crown Publishers. It covers in depth early crewel designs and the coloring that inspired these patterns.

Rose pink of the gentian family; bellflower of the bluebell family; or even Carolina spring-beauty of the purslane family.

Pinks or carnations of the dianthus family

Garden phlox of the phlox family

Potato vine of the morning-glory family or spotted winter-green of the pyrolacaea family.

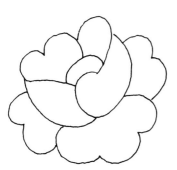

Traditional rose

Tudor rose

Pattern 84

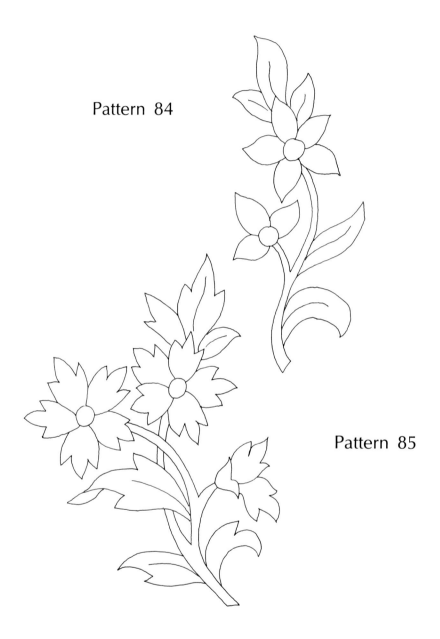

Pattern 85

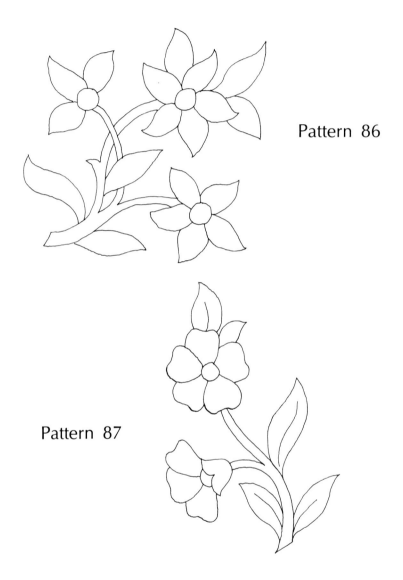

Pattern 86

Pattern 87

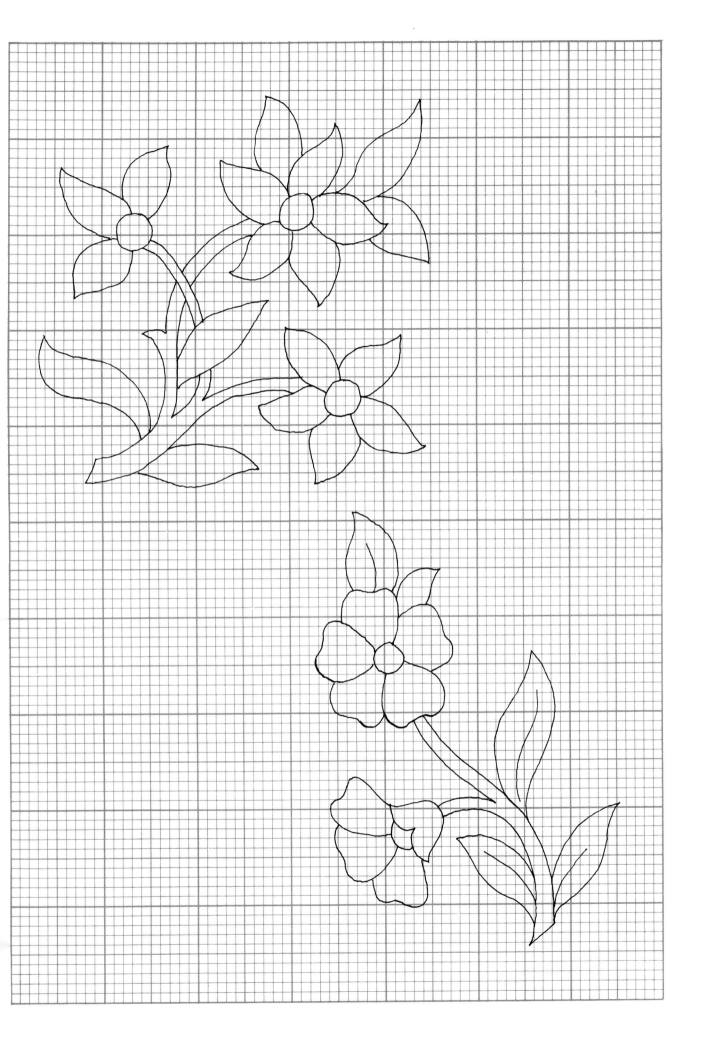

Pattern 88

Pattern 89

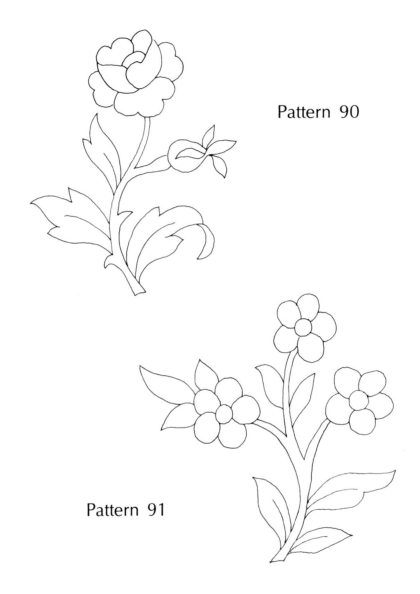

Pattern 90

Pattern 91

Pattern 92

Pattern 93

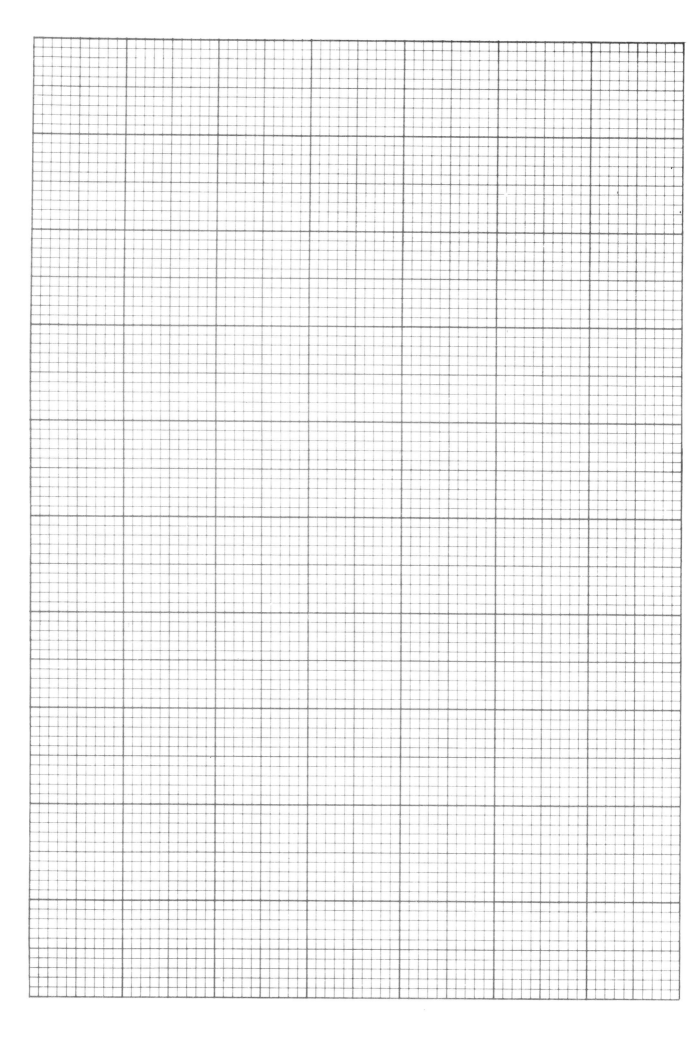

CHAPTER 10:

Combining Patterns

Now the real fun begins. It is time for you to combine patterns for a project of your own creation. To get you started, I have scaled down some of the patterns and created four projects. You, of course, will think of a million more possibilities.

There are two ways to combine patterns: You can take small sections from a pattern and combine them with sections from other patterns until you have a new composition, or you can take a pattern in its entirety and combine it with other complete patterns or repeat it so that you create a larger pattern from the same illustration.

The lily of the valley at the base of Pattern 2 is a portion of Pattern 12 that has been reversed. The lower left section of Pattern 12 is the right-hand base of Pattern 2. This is what is meant by using a part of one pattern with a part of another.

The following projects are samples of how complete patterns can be worked together to make larger designs. The drawings are reduced so that you can see the total effect but they are at scale with the original patterns in this book.

After you have chosen the flowers, decided where you want each of the blossoms, and selected what leaves you wish to use, go back and add the interconnecting stems and vines. You'll then have a lovely work for a chairseat, pillow, picture, or tablecloth. Don't let the idea of ''creating'' or ''designing'' intimidate you. It really is quite easy to do and you can plan it all out on tracing paper until it is just what you want. Use pencil so that you can erase those overlapping petals and leaves that you do not want in the final work. The easiest way to start is simply to plunge in and try it. I think you'll be delightfully surprised at your inventiveness.

Project 1

PROJECT 1

This project combines only two patterns: Pattern 19 and Pattern 57.

I began by drawing Pattern 57 full size on tracing paper. Then I flopped the tracing, redrew it in the opposite direction, and connected the foliage appropriately. It looked rather oblong and the bud in the upper right side of the central part looked a little out of place. I considered eliminating that bud to make the panel look more finished, but decided, instead, to add the rose bud from Pattern 19 to give a more elongated effect to the panel and connected the stem into the leaf of the lower wild roses.

The rose bud pattern seemed more suitable to the traditional rose pattern, but when I'd finished, it looked like it belonged. You might consider shortening the stem a bit, or perhaps eliminating the lower cluster of leaves and allowing the spray of leaves from the upper portion to drop behind the wild roses of the lower portion. I think this would make it more compact and, perhaps, just a little better.

Project 2

PROJECT 2

This project combines Patterns 58, 59, 60, and 18.

To make a long, willowy wildflower panel, I first used the lovely drawings from the Walcott paintings. The original panel had columbines at the top (Pattern 58), then wild pinks (Pattern 59), the painted trillium (Pattern 60), and finally, the white violet and lily of the valley (Pattern 2) at the base. The overall panel was thirty-six inches high and very spectacular. You might try it.

For the panel here I substituted sweet peas (Pattern 18) at the base to give more color variation and to allow the reds which predominate in the top columbine to be reintroduced at the base in the sweet peas. I also liked the idea of a vine at the base which seemed to anchor the panel to the ground.

Notice how each flower stem blends into that of the succeeding flower. You can lengthen or shorten them to fit your needlework within a restricted area such as a piece of fabric which is just "so big" or a chair back which is shorter than your original pattterns.

Use your own imagination and create a companion piece to this panel and see how easy it is.

PROJECTS 3 AND 4

I created these projects for a pair of twin-sized bedspreads. To completely cover the spreads would have been an enormous project, so I designed a series of florals at the base of the spreads just above where an extra blanket might be tossed.

Both projects include patterns from the mille fleur chapter only. Of course, the variations from just that section were enormous, so I rather picked the shapes that I liked and worried about the coloring afterwards. I often change the classic coloring of flowers if I think it will look better or suit the room more. You should think this way, too. Who cares if I make the iris yellow and the carnations pale pink instead of the original colors!

Project 3 is comprised of the following patterns: Pattern 66, strawberries; 74, clary; 75, pinks; and, 76, sow-thistle.

Project 4 combines Patterns 70, white violets; 81, carnations; 82, field daisy; and 83, iris.

I know you will be much cleverer than I in thinking up your projects. My hope is that this section and this book has given you the courage to set out on your own, the way our grandmothers did, and create a family treasure from your heart and with your own hands.

Project 3

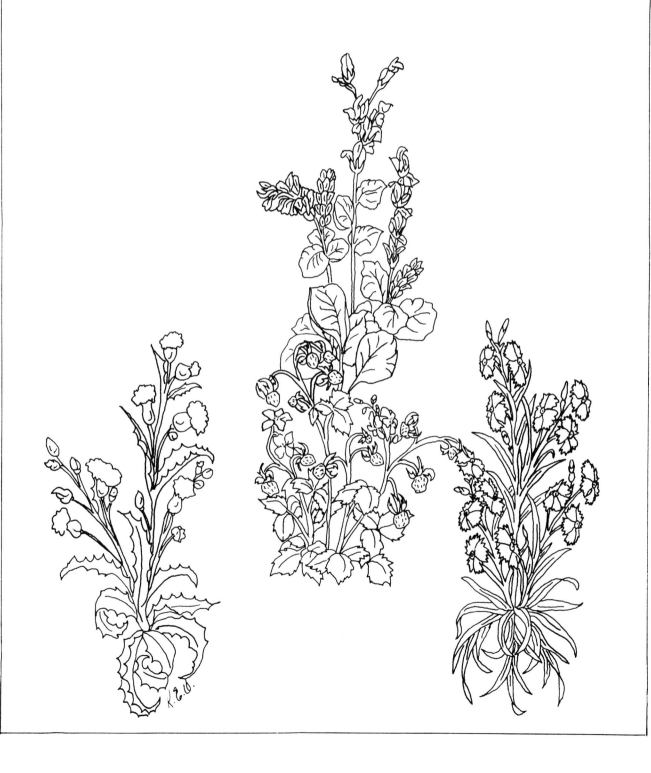

Project 4

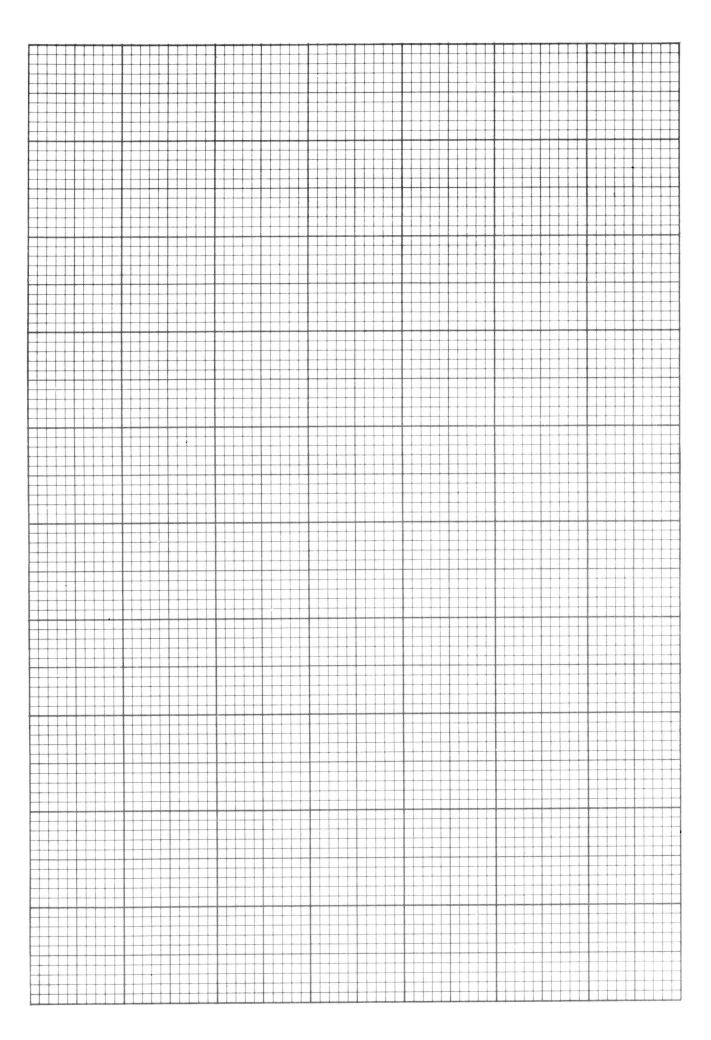

Glossary of Stitches

For the person who seeks out "art" in embroidery, the interplay between texture, color, and design is the essence of the whole thing. It is not so easily accomplished, but the pursuit of excellence and interpretation keeps us diving back into the "can of peanuts" for more.

The selection of stitches is as important in embroidery as the color. The stitches are the only true vehicle to texture in a three-dimensional art form such as crewel embroidery.

On the following pages you will find only a small selection—a primer really—of 88 stitches out of literally hundreds and hundreds. In illustrating the stitches, I have tried to simulate the texture which the stitch will give. Obviously, many stitches are left out and I suggest you seek out one of the many excellent books on just stitches for further development of your "vocabulary."

If I have goofed on one of the drawings, please let me know as there is a point at which all the lines in the illustrations seem to blend together when drawing. I would be tickled to hear from you. It is like getting caught with a spelling error after publication! Since this is our unique language, do let me know.

The following is an alphabetical list of the stitches covered in the Glossary. The numbers refer to the stitch number in the Glossary.

1. Back stitch

2. Back stitch, threaded

3. Bokhara couching

4. Braid stitch (posette)

5. Brick stitch

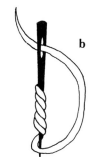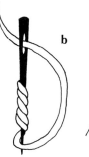

6. Bullion knot

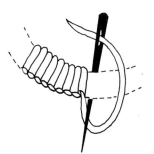

7. Buttonhole stitch

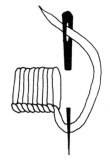

8. Buttonhole stitch, close

9. Buttonhole, closed

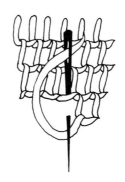

10. Buttonhole filling, spaced (attached)

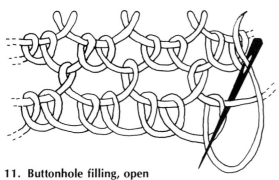

11. Buttonhole filling, open

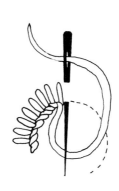

12. Buttonhole stitch, inverted

13. Buttonhole stitch, open

14. Buttonhole stitch, tailor's

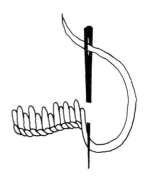

15. Buttonhole stitch, long and short

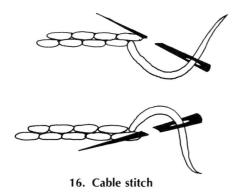

16. Cable stitch

17. Chain stitch

18. Chain stitch band, raised

19. Chain stitch, cable

20. Chain stitch, heavy

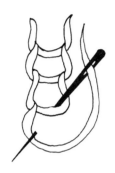

21. Chain stitch, open

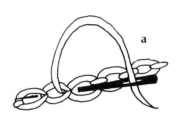

22. Chain stitch, threaded

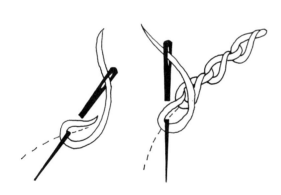

23. Chain stitch, twisted

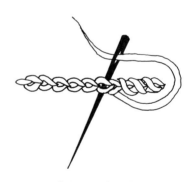

24. Chain stitch, whipped

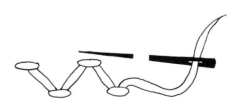

25. Chevron stitch

194

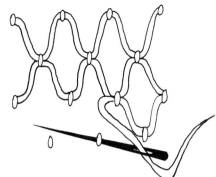

26. Cloud filling stitch

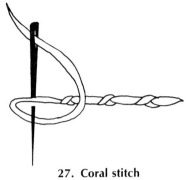

27. Coral stitch

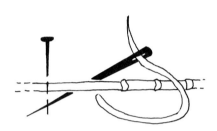

28. Couching

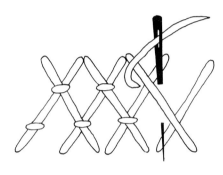

29. Couched filling stitch

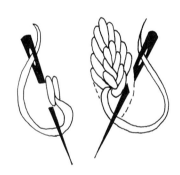

30. Cretan stitch

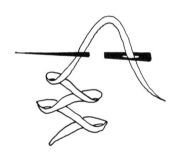

31. Cretan stitch, open

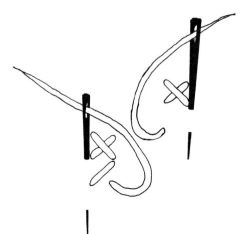

32a. Cross-stitch, vertical

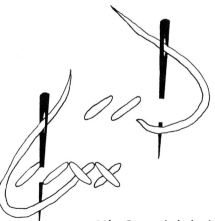

32b. Cross-stitch, horizontal

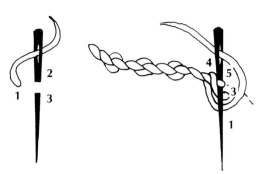

33. Double knot chain

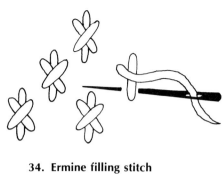

34. Ermine filling stitch

35. Feather stitch

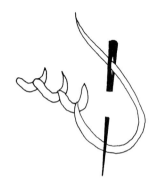

36. Feather stitch, single

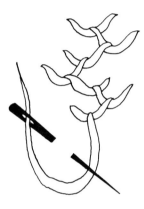

37. Feather stitch, double

38. Feather stitch, triple

39. Fern stitch

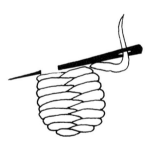

40. Flat stitch

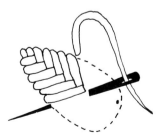

41. Fishbone stitch

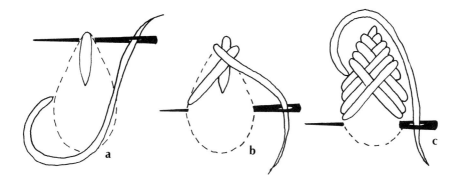

42. Fishbone stitch, raised

43. Fly stitch, single

44. Fly stitch, closed

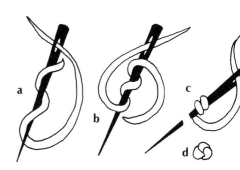

45. French knot

46. Herringbone stitch, open

47. Herringbone stitch, closed

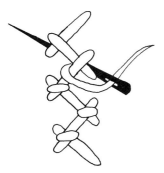

48. Herringbone stitch, couched

49. Herringbone stitch, raised

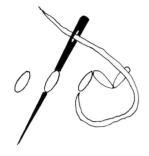

50a. Holbein stitch, angled

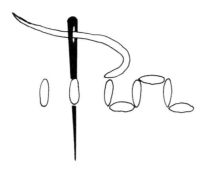

50b. Holbein stitch, squared

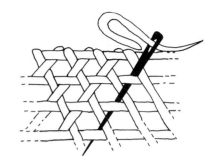

51. Honeycomb filling

52. Lazy daizy or chain stitch, detached

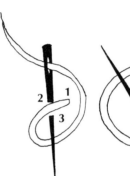

53. Knotted cable stitch

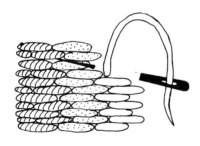

54. Long and short stitch

55. Long and short stitch, shaded and padded

56a. Outline stitch, stem stitch

56b. Outline stitch, crewel stitch

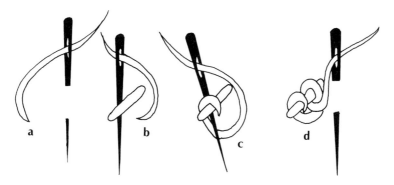

57. Palestrina knot

58. Pekinese stitch

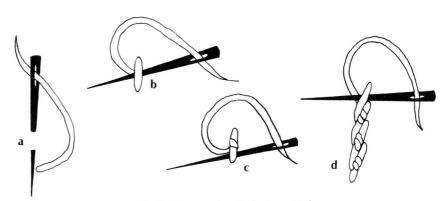

59. Portuguese knotted stem stitch

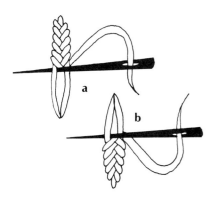

60. Raised needleweaving

61a. Raised stem band, vertical

61b. Raised stem band, horizontal

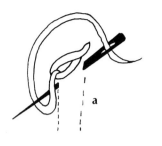 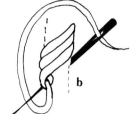

62. Rope stitch

 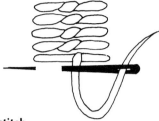

63. Roumanian stitch

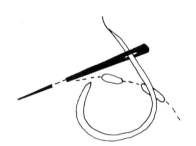

64. Running stitch

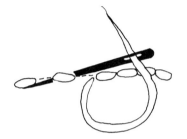

65. Running stitch, double

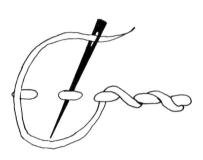

66. Running stitch, whipped

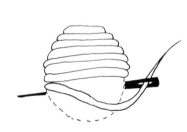

67. Satin stitch

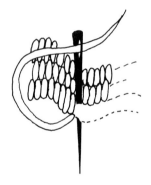

68. Satin stitch, blocked

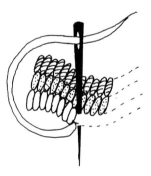

69. Satin stitch, blocked and shaded

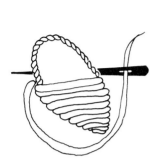

70. Satin stitch, padded

71. Satin stitch, split

72. Scroll stitch

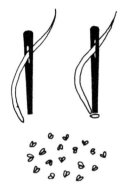

73. Seeding stitch

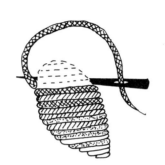

74. Shaded laid work

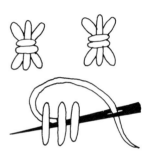

75. Sheaf filling stitch

76. Sorbello stitch

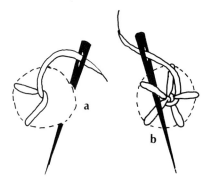

77. Spider web

78. Spider web, raised or Rose web

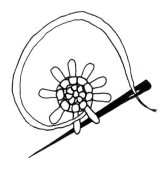

79. Spider web, whipped

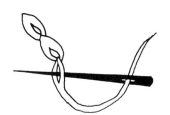

80. Split stitch

81. Star stitch

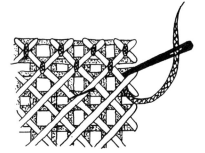

82. Squared filling, couched

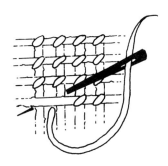

83. Trellis couching, basic or laid work

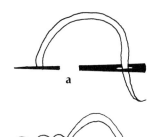

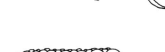

84. Turkey work

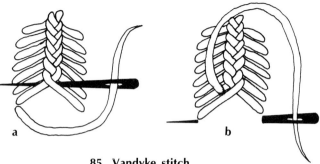

a   b

85. Vandyke stitch

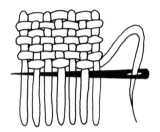

86. Weaving stitch

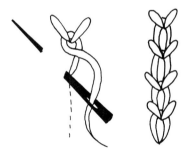

87. Wheat ear stitch

88. Wheat ear stitch, detached

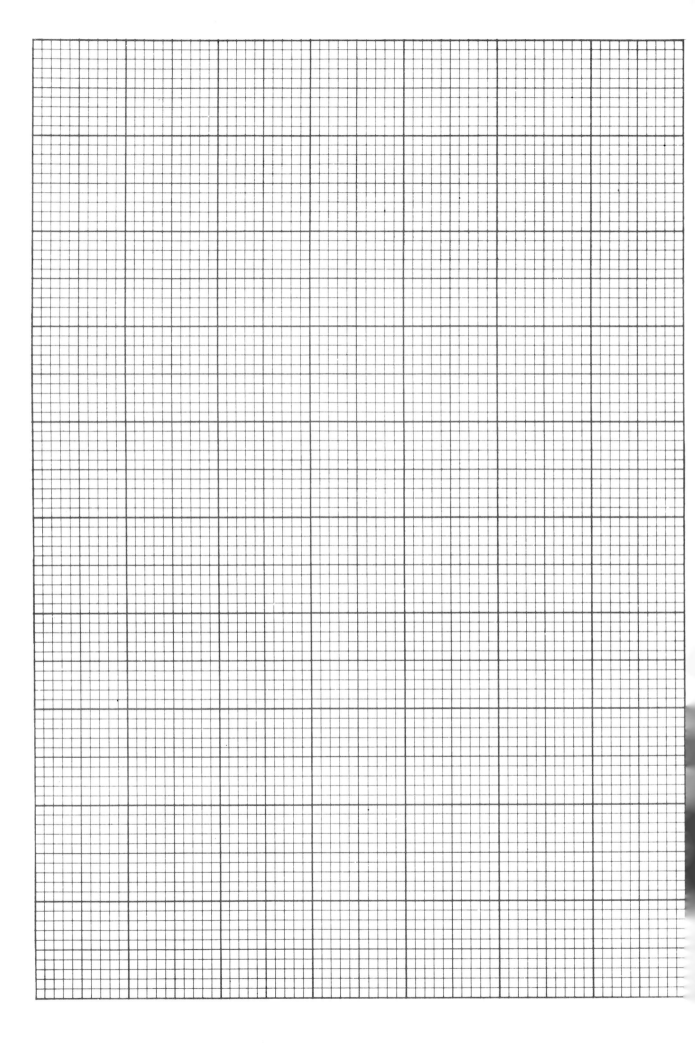

Bibliography

The books listed below are particularly good for colored pictures of flowers or are outstanding on the subject of color in the needlework arts.

Bagnasco, John J. *Plants for the Home.* Minneapolis: The Retail Group, Inc., 1976.

Bengtsson, Gerda. *U. S. State Flowers in Counted Cross-Stitch.* New York: Van Nostrand Reinhold Co., 1977.

Davis, Mildred J. *The Art of Crewel Embroidery.* New York: Crown Pubs., Inc., 1962.

Ferguson, Mary, and Saunders, Richard M. *Wildflowers.* New York: Van Nostrand Reinhold Co., 1976.

Freeman, Margaret B. *The Unicorn Tapestries.* New York: The Metropolitan Museum of Art, 1976.

Hay, Roy, and Synge, Patrick M. *The Color Dictionary of Flowers and Plants for Home and Garden.* New York: Crown Pubs., Inc., 1975.

Huxley, Anthony. *Mountain Flowers in Color.* New York: Macmillan Publishing Co., Inc., 1968.

Justema, William, and Justema, Doris. *Weaving and Needlecraft Color Course.* New York: Van Nostrand Reinhold Co., 1971.

Nicolaisen, Age. *Pocket Encyclopedia of Indoor Plants in Color,* edited by Richard Goren. New York: Macmillan Publishing Co., Inc., 1970.

Perry Frances, Ed. *Simon and Schuster's Complete Guide to Plants and Flowers.* New York: Simon and Schuster, Inc., 1976.

Pokorny, J. *A Color Guide to Familiar Flowering Shrubs.* London: Octopus Books, Ltd.

Walcott, Mary Vaux. *North American Wildflowers.* Washington, D.C.: Smithsonian Institution

Walcott, Mary Vaux, and Platt, Dorothy Falcon. *Wild Flowers of America.* New York: Crown Pubs., Inc., 1953.

Here are three books on ceramics and china painting which you will find invaluable.

Taylor, Doris W., and Hart, Anne B. *China Painting Step by Step.* New York: Van Nostrand Reinhold Co., 1976.

Thompson, Bill. *The Basics of China Painting.* Livonia, Michigan: Scott Advertising and Publishing Co., 1976.

———. *Fundamentals of Hobby Ceramics.* Livonia, Michigan: Scott Advertising and Publishing Co., 1976.

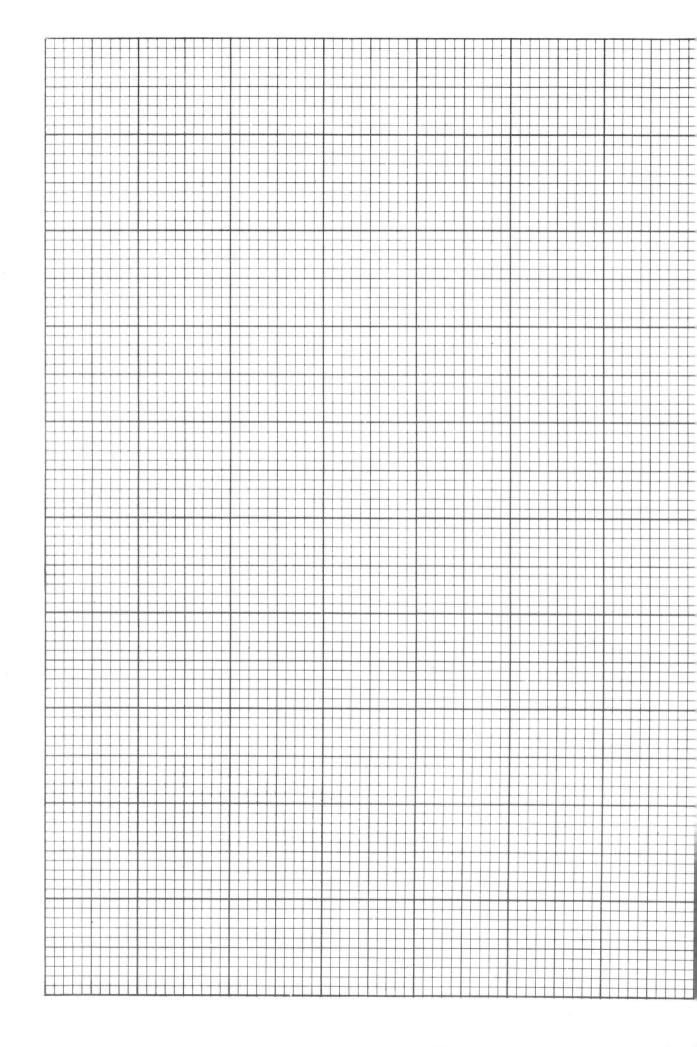

Suppliers

All materials mentioned in this book may be obtained by mail order from:
American Artisans, Inc.
C-5 Black Oak Drive #69
Nashua, NH 03060
Please enclose a self-addressed, stamped (#10) business envelope when inquiring for further information from American Artisans, Inc. If they do not carry an item, they will send you a current list of sources where you can obtain the specific materials.

SPECIAL SERVICES
Custom-made transfers in quantity (line work for crewel embroidery):
Simon Deighton/Alan Deighton
Deighton Transfers
56 Old Town
Bideford, North Devon
England

Course study in textiles and needlework including correspondence courses:
Mrs. Mildred Davis
American Institute of Textile Arts
Pine Manor College
400 Heath Street
Chestnut Hill, MA 02167
(The Institute can also give
you the names and addresses
of needlecraft schools and
courses in your area.)

Transpaints:
Freeman Transfer Printing Company
20 Catamore Boulevard
East Providence, RI 02914

Index of Flowers